D0007379

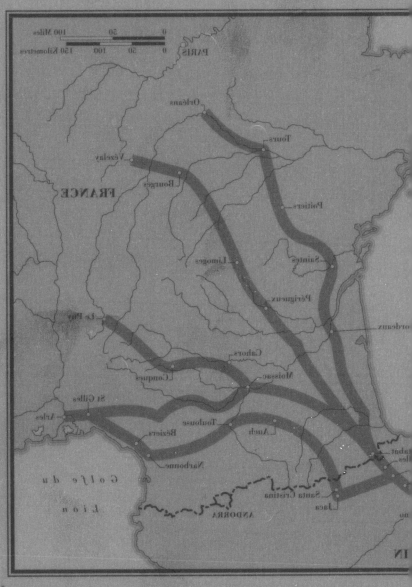

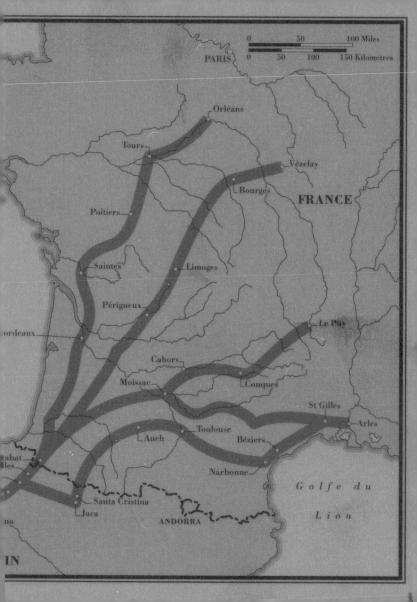

The Pilgrim Route to Santiago de Compostela

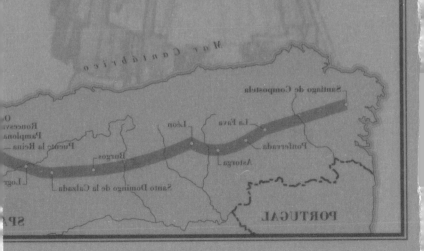

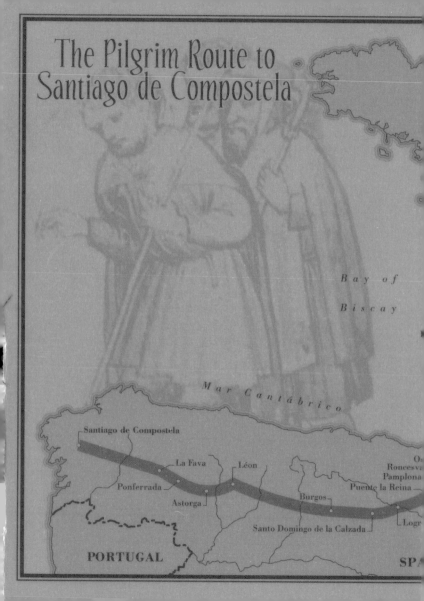

The Pilgrim Route to
Santiago de Compostela

Bay of

Biscay

Mar Cantábrico

Santiago de Compostela

La Fava

Léon

Ponferrada

Astorga

Os
Roncesva
Pamplona

Puente la Reina

Burgos

Logr

Santo Domingo de la Calzada

PORTUGAL

SP

On Foot to the End of the World

by
René Freund

Translated from the German by
Janina Joffe

 ArmchairTraveller

HAUS PUBLISHING
London

First published in Austria as *Bis ans Ende der Welt – Zu Fuß auf dem Jakobsweg* by Picus Verlag, 1990

Copyright © 1990 Picus Verlag, Wien.

This English translation first published in Great Britain in 2006 by Haus Publishing Limited, 26 Cadogan Court, Draycott Avenue, London SW3 3BX

A CIP catalogue record for this book is available from the British Library

ISBN 1-904950-42-6

Typeset in Garamond 3 by Jonathan Harley
Printed and bound by Graphicom in Vicenza, Italy
Jacket illustration courtesy of Getty Images

Spring 1999

There is a finished manuscript lying in front of me. Surrounding me are nearly five kilograms of notes: diary entries, receipts, brochures, shopping lists, packing protocols, letters, statistics, maps...

I will now banish all these piles of paper into a box and send the manuscript to the publisher. And then the Way-of-St-James-chapter will finally be closed.

I'm trying to document my experience of the journey to Santiago in this book. I'm using the word "document" because it refers to the fact that I have barely changed some of the documents – diary entries or letters – that I have drawn upon. I have done this because a literary reworking or a stylistic smoothing of these notes would have felt mannered and counterproductive.

I also did away with all too many bits of practical advice to the reader. First of all one can use detailed hiking guides for that purpose and secondly everyone walks the journey with his own two feet and sees it with his own eyes. Consequently, any hints or warnings only have a limited value.

So, now I will send the manuscript to the publisher and with that – no, the Way-of-St-James-chapter will not be closed. There is an old pilgrim's saying that I've only just recognised to be true: The journey doesn't end in Santiago. The journey begins in Santiago.

June 1998

How does one come up with the strange idea of walking on foot for two months to a cathedral one never even knew existed? Many pilgrims believe in providence and will simply smile when one tells them of "coincidences". I'm no great believer in a magical worldview because I believe that we humans create most situations for ourselves, but somehow things did seem a bit jinxed on our journey.

We – my wife Barbara and I – have always wanted to take a long trip but never quite knew when, how or where to.

At the wedding of two close friends I met a man who spent the evening telling me fascinating stories of his experiences on one of the oldest pilgrim routes in the world: the Way of St James to Santiago de Compostela. I not only found out a lot about the life of a modern pilgrim, but also about the history of the "Camino de Santiago", as the Way is referred to in Spanish. It is named after Saint James or James the Great, Sant Iago in Spanish, Saint Jacques in French. James and his brother John belonged to the "inner circle" of the Apostles. James was one of the first martyrs: he was beheaded around the year 44. Other than these facts, not much of what is known about him is indisputable. It is said that two of James's students took his body from Jerusalem to Galicia in western Spain, where the apostle had allegedly evangelised. There, James found his final rest – until either the year 813 or 825, no one knows for sure. In that year a pious recluse was led to the grave of the saint by a supernatural light over a field ("campus stellae", Starfield). To cut the story short, Santiago de Compostela arose as a result.

It is certainly no coincidence that the Reconquista began parallel to the cultivation of this legend; the Reconquista being the Christian reclaiming of the Islam-ruled Iberian Peninsula. This recapturing took time, from about the 8th to the 15th century. This was partly due to the fact that the population itself was satisfied with the Islamic-Moorish governance – Christians and Jews, for example, had complete religious freedom; the economy was flourishing; the first universities were being built on Spanish soil.

But then the Christian armies arrived (the first were allegedly led by Charlemagne) and the heydays of poetry, philosophy, science and tolerance ended. The Christians used this opportunity to not only eradicate most of the Moors but also the Jewish population. James was revered as a saint and a great warrior. He is still present in many old Spanish depictions as Santiago Matamaros ("moor killer") with a sword, on horseback, surrounded by the severed heads of dark-skinned, frizzy-haired enemies of Christianity.

It didn't take long for Santiago to become as famous a destination for pilgrims as Rome and Jerusalem. In 1078 the construction of a new cathedral began. Old books report a veritable pilgrimage boom between the 12th and the 14th century. Protected by a scallop shell sewn onto one's tippet, one would make a pilgrimage to the apostle's grave in order to express gratitude or wishes. There are also reports of pilgrimages ordered by judges as a punishment. Likewise, there were delegated pilgrimages made by professional pilgrims who were paid to travel to Santiago by the individual seeking help.

During the Reformation pilgrimage suffered a crisis. Erasmus of Rotterdam criticised the greed of the apostle (Santiago lived very well from the exploitation of the pilgrims) and Martin Luther ridiculed the followers of the "Compostel" cult, since "one doesn't know whether Saint James or a dead dog or a dead horse lies buried there…"

The confused stories surrounding Saint James didn't end there, though. In 1879 the apostle's grave was rediscovered, so to speak – because it had been forgotten where exactly it was. During digs in the cathedral some bones were indeed found: they were certified as undoubtedly those of the apostle by a papal bull. In 1937 General Francisco Franco helped make the apostle cult ultimately dubious by turning St James's Day (25 July) into the Spanish national holiday and naming St James the country's patron saint.

Today, pilgrimage is still extremely popular: In 1982 the Roncesvalles monastery at the beginning of the Camino de Santiago recorded 526 overnighters, in 1997 there were already 11,516. In the holy year 1999 more than twenty million pilgrims were expected in Santiago. (Every year in which St James's Day falls onto a Sunday, is considered a "holy year" and only in these years the "puerta del perdon" or "puerta santa", the eastern portal of the Cathedral of Santiago is opened. St James's Festival on 25 July is a great experience for all those who don't suffer from claustrophobia.)

Most of the pilgrims travelling the Camino these days are not walking it for strictly religious reasons. The Camino de Santiago has become a meeting place for all different kinds of people from all over the world, clearly doing justice to its description as "Europe's first road of culture". Even Goethe suspected that "Europe had come into existence through the pilgrimage to Compostela".

For an entire evening, the man at the wedding celebration told me the story of and many stories surrounding the Way of St James. He explained that there were four "classical" paths to Santiago: from Paris via Tours, from Vézelay via Limoges, from Le Puy via Conques, from Arles via Toulouse. Peter Lindenthal, as this man was called, had taken the trip on various different routes and is also the author of the highly recommendable book *On the Way of St James through Austria*.

The next morning my wife called me: I shouldn't be shocked, but our tenancy contract had just been ended by the landlord who wanted to move into the property himself in September. In response, I told her about the Camino de Santiago and almost simultaneously we came up with the idea that we should take advantage of our temporary "homelessness" in order to go, or better yet, walk on a two-month trip. It so happened that we came across a place to store our furniture and also realised that we only had very few and easily moveable appointments during October and November. So we decided to embark on our journey. We chose to start from Le Puy in the French Massif Central because this was the most "classical" of the routes and most suited to hikers.

September 1998
Packing list for my rucksack

1 rain cape; 1 Gore-Tex jacket; 1 rain protector for my rucksack; 1 cotton beanie; 1 wool jacket; 1 cotton jumper; 1 pair of long trousers; 1 pair of shorts; 3 t-shirts; 3 pairs of boxers; 3 pairs of hiking socks; 1 small towel; 1 pillow case (can be used for available pillows or be filled with clothing to make a pillow); 1 baseball cap; soap, shampoo, sewing kit, toothbrush, travel size toothpaste; 1 tube of *Hirschtalg* (an anti-blister ointment); 1 tube of hand-washing liquid; 1 passport; 1 tape recorder; 1 notepad; 1 ballpoint pen; money and credit card; 1 pair of leather hiking boots; leather conditioner for boots; 1 pack of plasters; 1 packet of tea bags; 1 pocket knife; 1 camera; 1 compass; 3 maps; 1 travel guide; 1 book; 1 sleeping bag; 1 flashlight; 1 water bottle; 1 walking stick (for support, pace keeping, protection from aggressive dogs, climbing over barbed wire fences, crossing streams or swampy areas, bending down branches or knocking down fruit, measuring water depths, hanging up washing).

Total weight of backpack: 10 kilograms.

Le Puy-en-Velay, 22 September 1998

Le Puy is a good place to begin a pilgrimage. In between steep, rocky mountains and hills, and the remains of extinct volcanoes lies the capital of the Departements Haute-Loire. To put it casually, there is at least one church, cathedral, chapel or enormous statue of a Madonna and child. Le Puy is undoubtedly a holy place; well, at least it was one once.

The woman in the cathedral's sacristy has already walked the route from Le Puy to Santiago three times. She made her last trip at age 74, after a serious hip operation. She explains kindly that we should have applied for an official pilgrims' pass at our local parish or one of the St James's societies – we think it best to keep the fact that we don't even have a local parish to ourselves. As consolation, she gives us a kind of tourist logbook in which we can collect stamps from each leg of the journey. She says that the official pilgrims' pass wouldn't be of any use to us in the Chemin de Saint Jacques, the French part of the Way of St James anyway, since most of the pilgrim hostels or *"gîtes d'étape"* belonged to the parish and in France state and church are admirably separated. In Spain however, one would need the pass in order to spend the night in the pilgrim hostels or *"refugios"*. Being an experienced pilgrim she explained to us that the hostels were of varying quality. They always had a shower, toilet and sleeping place, and some even had kitchen facilities that sometimes included kitchen appliances. Often one could also find basic foodstuffs such as oil or salt and spices, garlic or jams. If these weren't present, one should buy some to leave for the next guests. As a result there would always be a quiet sharing "exchange".

The old lady recommended the Couvent de la Providence, the Convent of Providence next to the Saint-Laurent church for our stay in the Le Puy. I wrote in her pilgrims' book: "Nous nous fions à la Providence" – we set our trust in providence, which, when you think about it, is really the only thing that's left to us in life. It's just that one notices it a little more as a pilgrim because one has to take the things one is given, whereas normally one can at least choose freely from the menu or the TV guide.

Bains, 23 September

Today we walked 15.5 km, a real beginners' achievement… but all right since we didn't want to overdo it in the beginning. Tomorrow we should walk at least 16.5 km. Then we would be in Monistrol-D'Allier where we could sleep, eat and shop. Or we add on another 12 km, making 28.5 km and we would be in Saugues, which also has a good "infrastructure", as we like to refer to the humble sleeping and shopping possibilities along the way. It is only our first night on the Way of St James and I can already make out what we will be spending most of our time doing: namely finding the best way to walk so as not to end in no-man's-land in the evening, since the nights are already far too cold to sleep outside.

During breakfast in the monastery at Le Puy we met a married couple, both around the age of sixty. They are French-speaking Canadians from Quebec and had already done the Spanish part of the route last year. "My backpack was twenty kilos," says Guy-Marie. "I already ruined my feet on the first leg across the Pyrenees, and after two weeks in Spain I told my

11

wife: I'm never doing such a crazy thing again in my entire life. Now, not even a year has passed and we're on our way again."

We lingered in Le Puy until noon, since it is a pretty town. Then we set off to climb onto the Rue de Compostelle and looking down onto the town breathlessly, we asked ourselves how on earth we would ever make the next 1500 km on foot. Our first set-back was followed immediately by another when we realised that there was no shop at the top of the mountain… so we headed back down to buy provisions. Fortunately, food shopping in France is always a great pleasure since even the smallest supermarket offers so many different types of cheese that one could eat three new varieties on every day of the month without repeating a single one.

But now to the important part: the Way! How beautiful this route is when one has finally left the outskirts of the city! It snakes its way through oak forests, over fields, along stone walls in which one can hear lizards scuttling. It leads through pine forests and past fat contented cows whilst always providing a beautiful view — hundreds of kilometres in any direction! I now know why I hesitated so long to describe this trail: I simply cannot do it justice.

Bains, 23 September

Dear Michaela!

Today we are staying with a family that also rents out guest rooms. Right now we are sitting in their living room, the mother is cooking, the daughter is doing her homework in the kitchen, and the son is unpacking his kit after football practice and going to have a shower. We are only two add-ons to the family but must nonetheless be a pain. We want tea, want to smoke and are sitting around uselessly. Bains is a small village with one hotel-restaurant where we were unwanted both for eating and sleeping. Someone told us it was because the owners were simply too lazy.

We have ended up in what seems to me the cosiest house in the whole place, with the Raveyre family, and this is where we will stay.

The weather was so nice today; we both got a bit of a sunburn. I suppose it also has something to do with the fact that we are normally around 900 m above sea level and the cool breeze prevents us from noticing the true strength of the sun.

See you soon! Yours, Barbara.

Monistrol-d'Allier, 24 September

Today, on our second hiking day, we have succeeded in getting lost for the very first time. It is a bit of an achievement, since the paths are labelled very well with red and white themed marking. A set of straight lines means the path continues straight ahead, a right angle means that the path is changing into another direction and a red and white cross marks the turns one shouldn't take. So it really is idiot proof.

Well, almost.

At least we have now learned one important piece of wisdom: if you are lazy, this laziness can often result in a more energy-consuming outcome; as for example when one doesn't return straight to the last signpost when one notices that there haven't been any for a while.

Aside from the stinging wind, which no one can

14

be blamed for, the path has once again done its best and adorned itself with little stone walls and forests and cows. One crosses large fields and then re-enters forests that could easily be in Styria. Along the way there are many fat stone crosses, reminding us that the route really is several hundred years old.

Above Monistrol there is an ancient St James's chapel with a wooden statue of the saint inside and a spectacular view outside. We looked through the "golden book" and found only effusive pilgrims thanking God, the Virgin Mary and Saint James for the beauty of the world and the joy of being able to walk the Way of St James. We thought for a long time but couldn't think of anything effusive to write. I'm afraid we just aren't holy enough yet. Or maybe we're just too tired. We haven't prepared for this amount of walking at all, neither physically nor mentally, which was probably not a good idea. As expected our feet are hurting, and our shoulders, and our legs; and our souls have to get used to this feeling of extreme vulnerability. It is feeling like we are exposed, bare and powerless on our trip. This notion is only underlined by our arrival in Monistrol-d'Allier. When we arrive the bakery is closed, half of the town looks like a building site and all of this is located in the deepest part of a shadowy valley. We quickly decide to make the climb to Saugues instead.

Saugues, on the same day

Although the weather is cooler in autumn, many fruits have only just ripened and prove to be excellent snacks. The blackberries we pick are so juicy they dissolve on our tongues and stain them black. We are extremely grateful for the abundance of berry bushes along the path because they give us a deliciously sweet excuse to stop for many breaks on the steep and tiring ascent to Saugues.

Here, we end up staying with Mrs Martin, who runs a kind of private pilgrim hostel which isn't cheap but very well kept. We consider Saugues to be much more welcoming than Monistrol and are very glad that we extended our day's travelling this far. Towards nightfall it did end up getting very dark so it was lucky that we hadn't yet heard the tale of the "bete du Gevaudan", an enormous wolf monster that today peers down onto Saugues in the shape of a wooden statue. The "bete du Gevaudan" killed over ninety people between 1764 and 1767 and its victims were exclusively women and children. The king sent out special units that hunted the beast for months with no effect. Today there is still debate about whether the giant wolf, which was finally killed by a local, wasn't perhaps a werewolf since it was so clever and versatile.

Of the twenty people eating with us in the hostel, the majority are pensioners who are only travelling a small part of the route accompanied by support vehicles. The food is very good: vegetable soup, roast lamb, cheese, dessert. In France, there is a minimum of four courses at every meal, even when one is basically eating with family.

As is often the case with pensioners, the dining room is as loud as a classroom. We spend time talking to Jean who is about 70 years old and walked the entire route last year. He explains that it took him about ten days on foot to realise why he was walking the Way of St James. "I thought I was walking the route because I was the best and most beautiful," he spoke open heartedly, "but then I realised that my reasons were much more simple than that." *Even more* simple than that? Well, he didn't reveal what they were, but we are already excited to see if we have a similar epiphany in ten days' time.

La Roche, 25 September

Today's journey would have been lovely if the weather had been better. We saw mysterious stone circles, beech trees with rotund foliage, enchanted oak groves and whispering streams – Ah, what lovely picnics we could have had in the shade, bathing our feet in the cool water! But instead we had rain accompanied by an icy headwind for the entire 22 km to La Roche. After our ten-minute lunch break with cheese and bread, in wool hats and windcheaters, we were completely frozen. Madame Jalbert, the woman hosting us in La Roche, points out that we have indeed been unlucky with the weather but actually had chosen a good time of year to take the trip. The trouble is that although spring is even nicer because everything is in bloom, this year there was still thick snow at Easter (after all we are at 1200 m above sea level). Then again, in the summer, it is often far too hot and there are the pilgrim caravans with twenty to thirty people stopping off in town every day. "It's too much work for me," Madame Jalbert points out. "I'm not sure I can go on like this much longer. Ten years ago there were hardly any pilgrims. Now there are more and more people every year!" We are sitting in her kitchen, drinking tea and watching her cooking. It makes us feel a little bit like children, sitting in grandma's kitchen.

"Nine days ago," Madame Jalbert excitedly reports, "there was a German girl here. She was about 25 years old, didn't speak a word of French, only slept here and didn't eat anything! She walked all the way from Monistrol to here in one go, that's almost 40 km! And the next she was off again at six in the morning, it was still pitch-black outside! Those Germans!"

Saint-Alban-sur-Limagnole, 26 September

Yesterday, I wrote that Madame Jalbert is a nice woman. It is, in fact, true, but why then has she sent us out of the house at eight o'clock in this dreadful rain? Today we established a new record distance: eight kilometres. Mind you, it only took us about one and a half hours, so we were actually very swift. It may be worth pointing out that there was no other day on the trip where we walked such a short distance or at such a high speed, ever again. It did rain many times on later occasions, but fortunately never as much as in those one and a half hours.

It wasn't rain that fell from the sky that day, they were water bombs that literally exploded against our *guaranteed waterproof* rain gear. Our trousers that were only covered by rain capes resisted the water for about ten minutes before they were saturated with cold moisture. Thanks to the wind that came at us from all angles they didn't just stay moist but became completely soaked. My waterproof and specially sealed leather shoes lasted for half an hour before filling slowly like the *Titanic*. Barbara's Gore-Tex shoes, which had been guaranteed as waterproof by a salesman ("You could wade through rivers with those and your feet would stay dry") suffered exactly the same way, but two and a half minutes after mine, and our special "climate controlled" socks experienced a complete climate breakdown. Our Gore-Tex jackets, however, only let water in where it could enter, namely at the openings of the sleeves and at the collar, and during particularly powerful gusts of wind, from the bottom opening. It was a complete disaster. The day before, in 6-degree weather and storm-like conditions, I had said that the weather couldn't possibly get any worse. When I turned around to what was left of Barbara today, which was merely a dripping, blue, hunched and hopeless-looking remainder of a rain cape, to tell her that *now* the weather really couldn't get any worse, she simply shuddered. She is now expecting a hailstorm for tomorrow. It may just be the very beginning of our trip to Santiago, but we have learned yet another lesson: if it is raining hard, you shouldn't set off in the first place because you end up ruining your feet in wet shoes. Morale sinks to an all-time low and you are left without a change of clothes because the rucksack shield doesn't really keep anything dry since it doesn't cover the entire backpack and isn't as waterproof as it claims to be. The scenery? Today it consisted of dripping blue Gore-Tex on both sides, a view of our hiking boots, asphalt, an occasional patch of field and the accompanying soundtrack was the beautifully rhythmic squish-squash squish-squash of our feet. Of course we also tried to hitch a ride from the four cars that passed us along the way, but as expected, drivers never stop when you need them the most. What is, in principal, a friendly openness towards pilgrims ends when it might result in the drenching of the beautiful velour seats in a fabulous new Renault.

Now we are in the café that along with the hotel and the restaurant belongs to the *gîte d'étape* in Saint-Alban-sur-Limagnole. Our soaking things have been left in the cellar's heating room and our not-so-soaking things are what we are wearing. Since we have sat down in the café, the sun has begun to poke out between the clouds. Nonetheless, we have no desire to continue walking today. We know that it would take us half a year to get to Santiago if we continued at *this* pace, and we had so much hoped we could be back home to celebrate Christmas ... but we just can't bring ourselves to put our wet gear back on. Instead we buy the big Saturday editions of the French newspapers, drink tea and watch the other guests in the café who are predominantly patients of the local Psychotherapy Clinic. They are observing us in return and I wouldn't be surprised if they thought we weren't entirely sane ourselves.

In Saint-Alban we have met three other pilgrims: one is a Swiss woman and the others are two men from Lyon. The Swiss woman is having an aperitif on the terrace. It's already dark and only 8 degrees outside but she doesn't seem in the least bit bothered. Henri is a recently retired school principal and Vélimir is a recently retired technician. He is originally from Dubrovnik and speaks French charmingly. Like us, Vélimir is sleeping in the large dormitory in the attic. Henri has booked his own room since he has caught a cold and wants a heater in his room.

Aumont-Aubrac, 27 September

I have now figured out why Henri took a single room. It wasn't because he got a chill, but because he simply wanted a good night's sleep! Vélimir's unbelievable snoring almost shattered my nerves and as a result we are staying in a real hotel room tonight.

It is raining outside and we are sitting on the bed eating bread and cheese watching the windows steam up whilst the wallpaper peels slowly off the walls. We couldn't stay in the "hotel bar" for long since it is really the family's living room and we got tired of hearing the mother pester her children about homework.

There is also a *gîte d'étape* that belongs to the hotel but it seemed awfully cold and miserable to us. Moreover, the hotel only costs a little bit more and rates are always charged by the room and not per person in France. Some of the Canadians we met in Le Puy have settled in the *gîte d'étape*.

Irma, the Swiss woman, overtook us during the daytime – she walks at more than 6 km/h. Henri and Vélimir have named her "Irma the terrible". What we have planned as tomorrow's entire day of walking is her afternoon walk today. Irma is a restaurant owner and has informed us that she is always available on her mobile phone. She started off in Zurich and isn't actually planning on going to Santiago. She wants to turn south at Burgos and walk as far as Malaga. "How come?" "I just *have* to walk," she says, and in her Swiss-German accent it almost sounds like a threat.

Today it only rained badly once, just as we were about to sit down for our lunch break. So we had our sandwiches on the go. I really don't mean to sound ungrateful since we did have some good luck today: the real hailstorm only began shortly after we arrived at our destination.

Montgros, 28 September

One feels like a true pilgrim on the "Aubrac" plateau: the landscape is rugged, there is a strong wind, it is very lonely and there is a lot of space for thought. In the Middle Ages the pilgrims feared the loneliness of the Aubrac: "*In loco horroris et vastae solitudinis*" as an old travel guide describes it. In the "Aux 4 chemins" bar, where there are indeed four paths joining together, there is a sign that reads: "Last oasis before the Aubrac". Even the locals consider the area to be desert-like. There are two men drinking pastis at the bar talking about the great wide world, as tends to be the case in places like this. They deliberate over how much a Ferrari costs in Italy and whether Battistuta is really a good football player or just a pretty face. They have already been expecting us and think we are "the Australians". Clearly the pensioners are ahead once again. It is often the case that you leave the hostel together in a group, but then split up because most people prefer to walk alone and most of the time it is just better to leave the pleasant rhythm of footsteps undisturbed by conversation.

In the morning we walked through the "Lower Austrian" part of the woods and even found a large porcini mushroom. In the afternoon we then arrived in the "Scottish Highlands". It rained the entire time but that is after all typical of those landscapes of the Aubrac. *"La pluie du matin n'arrête pas le pelerine"* is what Henri and Vélemir were singing this morning. "The morning rain does not stop the pilgrim."

Yes indeed, the morning rain also doesn't stop in the afternoon either. And yet we did truly enjoy this day of moorland scenery with its meandering brooks and occasional rock formations – bits of stone walls providing firm structure and the cows which soften the view with their expressive eyes.

Walking is very pleasant on this plateau, particularly when the clouds clear and you can see for hundreds of kilometres in all directions: you find a rhythmic pace, let the eyes wander (which is good when they have so much freedom of space!) and soon enough your thoughts are wandering at the same pace.

Even if you sometimes feel you could walk forever in this landscape, at some point your legs give in to tiredness. We finish our day in Montgros, which is good since "Chez Rosalie" is one of the loveliest *gîte d'étape* of the entire journey. It has terracotta floors, wood panelled ceilings, pretty tablecloths, massive wood furniture, an open fireplace... and you can detect Rosalie's personal touch in every little detail around the house. The pilgrim's menu is a little more expensive than normal, but it is substantially better.

We are served a hearty vegetable soup, a juicy roast, fresh vegetables, unique regional cheese and the special homemade pilgrim's cake.

We eat together with the Canadian couple and the two men from Lyon. Secretly we thank our parents for letting us learn French because this allows us to discuss the favourite pilgrim topics with the others: How can I make my rucksack lighter? While the Canadians even carry jam and honey with them in order to be independent at breakfast time, the men from Lyon are already prepared to send their sleeping bags back home. I managed to shock the group that included a teacher and a school principal by telling them that I had ripped my book in half yesterday and sent the finished half – weighing around 200 grams – to my sister.

Other popular topics among pilgrims include: What is that hostel like? Where did you get good food? As well as: Which walking technique is the best? We have also noted that absolute no-go areas are: Why are you walking the route? What are you expecting from the journey?, and any other metaphysical or existential questions. *"Ça ne se fait pas,"* ("One doesn't do that") Vélimir pointed out.

Later on, Rosalie's picture-perfect cook with his moustache, belly and apron explains why we are having trouble understanding the locals when they speak to us in French. It is in fact not really French, but "Langue d'oc" or "Occitan", an ancient language that is dying out. It is the language the troubadours once wrote in and in this remote area it has been preserved particularly well. "Hardly anything has changed here in centuries," our host tells us. "Hardly anyone new has moved here or gone away, so even the younger generation still speaks Occitan."

We are not only struck by the difference in language, but by another French speciality that we have only encountered in Paris: namely that in these parts everyone is extremely polite. When entering the bakery one says: "Bonjour Monsieur." The woman at the post office should be addressed with: "Bonjour Madame" and the people at the bar with "Bonsoir Messieurs-dames". If one walks past a lady and a gentleman on the street one nods politely and says,

"Madame, Monsieur". And even in the news, politicians' names are read as "Madame Albright" and "Monsieur Jospin". That amount of extra attention is simply a necessity.

Saint-Chély-d'Aubrac, 29 September

Today: Beautiful weather! Because we were so high up, at 1368 m, we even got slightly sunburnt, which we are almost happy about. We really enjoyed all of today, including the heath and pasture landscapes of the plateau, the view into the Lot valley and the coffee break in the afternoon sun in the town of Aubrac. On top of it all the *gîtes d'étape* in Saint Chely is fantastic as well. The Canadians have already made a fire in the open fireplace and to our great pleasure we even have our own little room. In the evening we cook spaghetti in the communal kitchen. Then we sit around the fire with the others and listen to Canadian Guy-Marie and Veronique's anecdotes about the Spanish part of the route. "It was beautiful!" Guy Marie exclaims. "We suffered sooooo much!" When we ask whether this isn't a contradiction they reply with shining eyes:

"One has to suffer, it is very important!" The two are very Catholic. The German woman who has been walking ahead of us like a phantom has immortalised herself in the hostel's guest book: "I felt very much at home here (by the open fire) for one evening of my long journey. Thank you very much. Ultreïa, Ursula (Hof, Bavaria -> Santiago)". Ultreïa is an old Latin pilgrim's greeting and means "always keep going" or "continue on". And Hof is, incidentally, on what used to be the eastern border of Bavaria and very far away from Saint-Chely-d'Aubrac.

What goes on inside your head when walking? When we ask each other what the other is thinking along the way, the other normally answers: "Oh nothing." And that is just about right. The path is a path into the present. One soon discovers that not being present can lead to mistakes – getting lost, missing sign posts, forgetting to refill water bottles…In the same way that we have sent home unnecessary extra weight by post, all unnecessary thoughts have been filed somewhere into the back of our brains. Along with them went any kind of "lofty" insights or philosophical revelations.

To be a pilgrim is an entirely un-intellectual experience. Perhaps that is why it has come back into fashion in our brain-focussed society. At some point everything simply falls away from you. All you want is to arrive and be underway at the same time. Walking is the form of travel most suited in pace to perception. You measure the world step by step, your breath adapts to this movement and a rhythm is created. It is the rhythm of motion, and motion is life – the ancient Greeks already knew this and liked to stroll as they philosophised. Thoughts are formed anew at this pace without us being aware of it, and without us being able to force it. Whenever you walk, you automatically gain instrospection.

Estaing, 30 September

Today the candle we just sent home to minimize rucksack weight would really come in handy. The light I am writing by this evening is particularly dim because it is coming from the fire. The large fireplace is, in fact, the only nice thing about this large communal hostel. The dormitory is about as charming as a hospital ward. If I had to stay here with forty others in the summer, I would rather sleep outside in the open air. But today the only other person sleeping over is Katharina from Swabia, with whom we have begun to speak in German, since we discovered that she is "Allemande". We already know her from the "Pilgrim's Post" that is passed from one hiker to the next. She is the one who was drying her trousers in the oven at the *gîte d'étape* in Aumont-Aubrac.

We spent half of today walking through chestnut forests. We gathered bags full of chestnuts which are now slowly roasting by the fire. On top of that – it happens to be harvesting time – we found two large porcinis which we are also frying. The red wine has, of course, been opened too.

Katharina is telling us that she walked the entire Way of St James from Le Puy to Santiago ten years ago when she finished secondary school. She is currently on holiday and only walking the stretch between Le Puy and Conques because she found the first two weeks of the journey had the most beautiful landscapes (which we can only confirm in retrospect). Katharina tells us that many people on the path have reached a cross-roads in their lives – they are thinking about divorce, changing careers, relocating. The last time she was on the route she was also in a situation where she didn't know how to continue. This time around she is happy not to be burdened with anything at all.

The descent from Saint-Chely-d'Aubrac to Saint Come-d'Olt involves a lot more climbing than I had expected. One really can't make the simple calculation that going from 800 m to 380 m will be smooth and relaxed. It took us five hours to walk those 16 km – but that may also have been the result of us having to eat so many blackberries along the way. In Saint-Come-d'Olt (Olt being a strange Occitan anagram for the name of the river Lot), a picturesque village built from grey stone, we drank a café crème and thanked Saint James for only letting it rain a little bit: *"une pluie correcte"*, "a correct amount of rain", as Henri put it this morning.

The next place we come through is Espalion, a real town. The bridges crossing the Lot and the houses standing along the wide calm river will remain among the most unforgettable of the journey. I would have loved to look at them longer, but the hostel in Espalion is actually outside the town and unfortunately also in the wrong direction. So we walked on towards Estaing, which can definitely compete aesthetically with the aforementioned locations. On the way we were surprised by a fierce thundering downpour and even more surprised when a driver stopped to drive us the last kilometre to Estaing.

We only found out later that one of the "legends" of the route lives in Estaing: he is named Dr Leonard and sold his successful practice after walking the Way and moved here with his family to give shelter to pilgrims. Everyone staying with him receives a bowl of soup and a bed, and if necessary some medical advice or encouraging words. We had heard so many stories about Leonard along the way that we were truly sad not to have visited him, but this way we met Katharina and that was worth it as well.

Espeyrac, 1 October
We are sitting in the dining hall of a slightly dilapidated

hotel and drinking the regional speciality "Gentiane", a bittersweet gentian liqueur. It tastes horrible, but for some reason proves to be very addictive. In other words: drinking it is like sitting in a sauna. You suffer but it is still enjoyable. We also suffered a great deal on our walk today, even though it was only 25 km – but 4/5 of which were on asphalt. "It just makes your feet flat," Katharina notes in her Swabian accent, and she is totally right. The last hour before Espeyrac was the worst because we had to walk downhill in the pouring rain which meant our feet were slipping backwards and forwards in our shoes all the way. Our morale sank as our blisters grew, and it had all begun so nicely walking along the Lot promenade – a long broad river with a few colourful leaves drifting in it can be very uplifting for the spirits. Around lunch we bumped into Katharina again and round about that time it began to rain heavily again. I think the rain can sometimes cloud your view of roads, villages and landscapes to make their beauty drown completely. Perhaps that is why we found Golinhac and Espeyrac so particularly dreary. Katharina is staying in the parish's *gîte d'étape* in which everything is broken but also free. The hostel has a boarded-up shower, old hospital beds, mould on the walls and a beautiful garden. Since we won't be needing a garden today we have decided to stay in a 0-star-hotel where we can at least dry all of our clothes.

Katharina visits us for dinner and orders the same all-inclusive menu as us, which includes a hotpot that tastes of fish even though it contains no fish. Outside it's raining even more than usual, which pleases us since two days ago Henri told us that: "The rain that comes down today won't come down tomorrow." Whilst discussing the philosophical implications of this statement we receive a weather forecast predicting another rainy front, which at least sounds elegant in French: *"Une nouvelle zone pluvio-instable attaint le pays..."*

It is said that the pilgrims used to follow the Milky Way on their path. Buñuel also made a film about the Way of St James called *"La voie lactee"*. All I can say is that we wouldn't have gotten far using the Milky Way Method in this awful weather.

Espeyrac, 2 October

We are sitting in exactly the same way as we were last night with Katharina, but now we are having breakfast. She also has some words of wisdom to offer us: "Complaining enough makes you half satisfied" (which sounds even wiser in her Swabian accent). That is exactly why we have been complaining for the past hour about the dreadful weather that is even worse than yesterday. I mean, I didn't free myself of work commitments for two months in order to hang around in terrible hotels in grey villages waiting for the rain to stop. And so we keep complaining and complaining and things do improve – not the weather, but our spirits. So we get tired of complaining, put on our chilly, damp rain gear and step out into the rain.

Conques, 2 October

The rain only stopped once on our way to Conques, when the storming wind blew the heavy clouds out of the way for a few minutes. Today we experienced first hand, and rather intensely, why the French word for pilgrim (*pelerin*) is so similar to the word for a rain cape (*pelerine*). Today I also broke my hiking stick/ pilgrim's staff. I got it from my mother's garden and it was made of beautiful hazel wood that I had dried and crafted lovingly. We were crossing a stretch of asphalt, completely soaked, my back aching from the weight of my rucksack when, as if to mock me, the icy wind lashed straight into my face, then onto my legs from the left and finally bit into my bare neck from behind. I began to scream and curse Saint James and all other saints that came into my mind as well. I got myself into such a rage that I began violently thrashing about with my stick, screaming at the elements that I was in fact a Protestant – and not even a real one – and that I wanted nothing more to do with this miserable pilgrimage business. In that moment my stick shattered on a bit of fencing and I continued breaking up the leftover pieces and hurling them into the countryside – and I felt a lot better. For one I wasn't burdened with carrying it around anymore and looking rather venerable, but also slightly lame like St Nicolas. For another I can now put both hands in my pockets or let them hang down and move like a modern human being instead of a visitor from the Middle Ages.

Conques is great. Everything here is old, so old in fact that one can hardly determine anything about the actual origins of this town. It lies in a wooded valley virtually stuck to the slope of the hills around it and really there appears to be no aesthetic or practical reason for choosing precisely this place to build such a magnificent yet simple church and such a monumental yet plain monastery. And still, more than a thousand years ago workers began placing one brick upon another until a few hundred years and many lives later the whole thing was finished. Then, in 1130, a great master came and chiselled "The Last Judgement" into the stones above the church portal. With that he created one of the most famous Romanesque sculptures central Europe has to offer. It is interesting that, like in most representations of "The Last Judgement", the portrayal of Hell is far more lively and accomplished than that of Heaven. In Hell there is so much screaming and torture and burning and violence and fornication and gluttony and suffering that it is almost pleasing to the senses. In Heaven, everyone is just standing around together decorously staring into space looking a tad bored. But how *can* one depict Heaven accurately? Let's hope that it isn't really that boring in reality.

We decided to spend the night in the monastery. We climbed endless stone and wooden steps higher and higher until we reached an immaculately renovated attic room. We then spent the afternoon exploring all the tiny corridors, hidden doors and back rooms of the monastery. There was a hint of *The Name of the Rose* in the air, but fortunately we didn't find any corpses lying around.

Naturally, there are many legends about the origin of Conques. Many of them had the purpose of defending the town's claim to power against competing abbeys such as Figeac. The stories revolved mostly around money, gold and land rather than God but when one is walking through the streets, church and monastery one can still feel that religion was once extremely important to people here. What many

41

people now look for in eastern religions because they feel it is missing from Christianity can still be sensed here – the spirit and the spirituality. In Conques, this spirit is closely tied in with the Way of St James. Not only because of the constantly recurring images of the symbolic scallop shell but also because of the daily liturgy that is directed specifically at pilgrims and includes a pilgrim blessing every morning at 8 o'clock.

Even our hosts, who belong to the *Ordo Praemonstratensis*, seem extraordinary to us. They are warm, curious and open. Unlike most monasteries there are relatively many young monks here. We can tell from their many different activities that they are also hardworking businessmen. I also overheard that they love drinking wine and are clever at bargaining with their suppliers. And although they are busy with so many other things, we enjoyed their mass most out of any along our journey. It took place after the dinner and I gladly recommend the *Ordo Praemonstratensis* cuisine to anyone.

We had dinner with other pilgrims (including the

Canadians) and were served by an older couple who have been volunteer helpers here for two weeks. They have walked the route three times already. "There is a great danger that when one walks the route, home feels too claustrophobic afterwards." That is why they take trips on foot every year – through Spain, India and most recently Vietnam. And what is more, they add, everyone who has walked the route returns to it at some point.

We are told that evening mass will take place at 8 o'clock. We are rather reluctant to accept this invitation, but the devotion and power of the monks' songs enchants us in the end. This magical atmosphere is only enhanced by the fact that the entire church is lit only with candles. After mass the same father who before had negotiated the buying of the church's wine sat down at the enormous organ and played a half-hour improvisation on a Bach theme during which I almost felt like the church would take off and soar on a little trip around the universe.

Livinhac-le-Haut, 3 October

Our morning hike was harsh but we were rewarded

43

with a marvellous view of Conques when we finally arrived at the Sainte-Foy. From here Conques looked like a strange relic from another time. A word of advice for all those with eye problems: below the chapel there is a miraculous spring flowing out of a stone which is said to cure poor vision if one believes in it enough.

After the ascent we reached a high plateau from which we had yet another fantastic view that reached many hundreds of kilometres in all directions. At this point two immaculately-dressed Swiss men caught up with us. They belonged to a group that is doing part of the route on foot and a part by bus. They introduced themselves as Mr Beck and Mr Breu: names that should really be in a Dürrenmatt play. Mr Breu told us about "a pretty boy" named Marco from the Italian part of Switzerland who is also walking to Santiago. Mr Breu had taken him to dinner in Conques. Marco had completed an apprenticeship as a toolmaker but that wasn't enough for him – he wanted something else from life. And so he had obtained a Latin pilgrim's pass from his local parish. Mr Breu added that after the conversations they had had, he wouldn't be surprised if Marco began studying theology after his return from Santiago.

When we stopped for lunch after two hours together, the two Swiss men continued on after saying goodbye and we never saw them again. It is strange how many people you meet along the way, nice people, whom you lose out of sight so quickly. Even Katharina went home yesterday.

We found an entry made by Marco in the chapel notebook at our next stop a few hours later. He already seems like an old acquaintance to us. Maybe Mr Breu's prediction about a theology degree was right: the Franciscan motto *pax et bonum* has been laconically drawn above his name.

The other news we have is that there is no rain! Not even a drop! It was fantastic! We could simply walk over the tops of hills enjoying the view and it was almost saddening when we had to return into the valleys below. Not just because we knew that going down means we would have to climb up again, but also because the valleys are never quite as pretty. Decazeville for example isn't exactly a beauty. It lies directly in between a huge hospital and a huge cemetery. It is actually called La Salle and had to take on the name of a minister of industry in the 19th century. Now industry has hit rock bottom and hopelessness has remained. So we decided to continue walking to Livinhac. The hostel is particularly clean, which we have Ursula from Hof/Bavaria to thank for. She has written to us: "Hello, I got here very early. It was raining outside and I didn't know what to do with myself so I started cleaning the *gîte d'étape*." We met John and Cecilia from Scotland here. John has just retired from being the chief forester over the majority of woodland in Scotland. He was of course very confused when I asked him if there even were any forests in Scotland.

Of course there are forests. Lots of them.

We prepared for dinner while John and Cecilia told us about the adventures they had on the Spanish part of the route they hiked last year. One of their key observations was that everything is far cheaper in Spain than in France. Later we all went about our business individually: reading, writing, studying maps or cracking nuts. Yes, John and Cecilia spend the day collecting the nuts that lie around by the kilo, unused and free for the taking. "What a waste," John mumbled into his beard over and over shaking his head. They are cracking the nuts to reduce their weight and volume and putting them into plastic containers. They are already carrying at least 2 kilos of nuts with them and plan to take them home to make nut cake from them. "You see," said John winking, "we Scots are considered to be pretty economical."

La Cassagnole, 4 October

To me the Scots will now not only be remembered as being economical, but also very loud at snoring. Although Vélemir still gets the prize for being the loudest, the volume that John filled the room with was something else. It's funny because Barbara just turned over and *slept* like a baby while I spent half the night awake hearing every sound in the room. These long autumn nights are so torturous! I always try to fall asleep first so that I don't have to hear anyone else, but because I'm trying so hard I'm always the last one awake. Then I try to overhear the snorer but that only results in me hearing *only* the snorer. Then I try to stop him and his subconscious by making noises, but that just seems to encourage him to snore even louder. Then I try to pray. And finally I'm sitting upright in bed ready to cry. So in the end I got up, took my sleeping bag and slept on the kitchen floor. What heavenly peace!

At breakfast John told us that last year in Spain a very young and beautiful pilgrim had woken him in the night whispering "John! John!" He had already had his hopes up for what was to come when she added: "*Please* stop snoring!"

It only rained a little bit today so we could fully enjoy the oak woods, nuts, figs, grapes and blackberries. We had our lunch break under a protective barn roof with the Scots who were already there. They then took the longer route that is marked on maps for pilgrims because it takes them as far away as possible from French roads. Normally this is very enjoyable, but we wanted to avoid those muddy paths and instead took the direct route by the name of *Route departementale 2* and it was good that way. It meant we had time to have a coffee in Saint-Felix and were still faster than John and Cecilia. Saint-Felix is one of those places where even cemeteries die slowly. But there is no such thing as a village that is too small to be missing a memorial to the dead which shows just how populated it once was. It is shocking to see how many names are listed under that dates 1914–1918 next to the names of the most gruesome battlefields: Verdun – Somme – Marne… Similarly shocking is an additional plaque on the monument reading "12 May 1944" and underneath *"Fusillés"* (shot) with a list of men and women and next to children their ages: "8 ans"; "12 ans". No wonder old people in France aren't particularly warm towards the Germans and Austrians.

In the afternoon we decided not to go to Figeac but walk a little further. Not that we were particularly tempted to walk for 31 km but we didn't really feel like being in a town and everything is shut in most French villages on Sundays (and even Mondays in the smallest places). We heard later, that Figeac is beautiful, but then so is the *gîte d'étape* in La Cassagnole. It is privately run by a female calligrapher and her

taste and sense for details is visible in her minimal-
ist Japanese wall hangings and room dividers. There
is a kitchen full of food in a separate house with a
little till where you simply leave the amount which
you owe. But the best thing of all is that the Scots
have got their own room upstairs with a real door to
separate us. Between the two houses is an old linden
tree with garden furniture underneath. If it were 25
degrees rather than 7 degrees it would be lovely to sit
there, enjoying the view and drinking a bottle of the
house red. Instead we have linden-blossom tea in the
kitchen and that isn't half bad either.

Cajarc, 5 October

The guest book in our hostel reads: "2 October. On
today's journey I already collected half of my dinner.
Grapes, rosehip, walnuts, peppermint and fresh figs
made this rainy just a little more enjoyable. Added
to that I even found half a bottle of red wine in the
fridge – life is actually wonderful! I'm now going
to bed warmed up and happy. Ursula (Hof/Bavaria
-> Santiago)." One day later and with remarkably

50

different handwriting it says: "I'm back! Maybe it was the red wine, but I confidently followed the markings and promptly left town in completely the wrong direction. I then walked the variant route in the evening and got lost as a result. If someone had seen my temper tantrum I would have been delivered to the loony bin straight away. So, after my initial shock I have returned here. After my extra lap, I am having a coffee and then starting on my second attempt. Ursula".

Thanks to Ursula we were spared that mistake on our journey...

We arrived in Cajarc, incidentally where Françoise Sagan was born, after 25 km to find that by pilgrim standards it is nearly a metropolis. But first to our journey: there was hardly any rain and it was possibly one of the most beautiful stints yet. No climbs, endless pastures and after those came woods made of small withered oaks, a few birch trees, a lot of moss and fern. It looked so magical that we expected elves to leap across the path at any minute, or at least a wild boar.

But instead a fighter jet flew across the sky above us heading southwest. It would take a jet less than an hour to get to Santiago and we still have six weeks ahead of us. We are walking anachronisms.

We ate fluffy omelettes with fresh bread in Beduer and drank coffee in Grealou in the afternoon so I must note that hiking infrastructure was good. And Cajarc! There was already a supermarket at the beginning of the town. It's a pathetic provincial "Ecoprix" but still a huge temptation to us since we have wanted to do a proper food shop for quite some time. But of course we realise that this is all terribly inconvenient since we cannot carry anything more and all the packaging is even less useful when it comes in three-packs of chocolate or six-packs of yoghurt. This would mean either abstaining or stuffing our faces. So we decide on the latter.

We share our hostel with the Scots again because once you find companions you normally stick together until someone takes a break for a day like the Canadians or the men from Lyon. Alternatively you can run away from them, but we are not capable of doing that. But we learned something new, namely that we could have bought red wine for seven francs instead of the twenty we paid – "what a waste". We also learned that the Scots really don't wear anything under their kilts. After their bottle of wine John tells us that there is a video of his brother bungee-jumping that shows very clearly that Scots normally don't wear anything under their kilts.

Limogne-en-Quercy, 6 October

No rain, pretty paths, a lovely day. As usual the Scots were waiting for us in the *gîte d'étape*. We inspected the mattresses and showers, showered, shopped, cooked, ate and studied our route for tomorrow. It is strange how our way out of patterns repeated every day can turn into a routine very quickly.

Marco has been here too: *pax et bonum* it says in his unmistakable handwriting along with some other gushing text about how walking is turning into a rush for him and his feet are already carrying themselves to Santiago. Maybe it's just because we are so tired today, but somehow we are worried about Marco. He is all alone, with no one to balance out his thoughts and he might just be getting carried away and lifting off completely. Maybe one day he'll meet Ursula – the effusive God-seeker and the down-to-earth German – what a combination! After all, they are only one day away from each other. Funny how we think so much about people we don't even know.

Vaylats, 7 October

Despite the icy wind, there was no rain today and the walk was very nice. But we have started wondering if the oak woods will ever end. In the village of Bach we lay down on benches in the church and immediately fell into a deep sleep for half an hour. I'm sure it would be good for us to have one rest day a week like the others, but somehow we are too impatient and just want to keep going. The price we pay is this state of exhaustion. They really aren't huge distances, but the body just isn't used to walking for days on end.

After our church nap we had the choice of either crossing the "Bois du Grezal", a lonely stretch of forest feared by medieval pilgrims, for four hours in order to arrive at a *gîte d'étape* that may have been closed or to take a minor detour via Vaylats. We were told that there was also a monastery there were we could spend the night. Since the wind suddenly started picking up we decided on the monastery. Thank god! The nuns who call themselves "Filles de Jesus" received us very warmly and gave us a lovely room with a heater. This is not only comforting on cold days like this one, but essential for drying clothes. We get as excited about heated rooms as one would about winning the lottery – that's how rare they are. Apparently even the people who live in the south assume it will always be warm.

Vaylats, 7 October
Dear Michi!

I'm sorry I haven't written for so long, but in the past few days we have either stayed up late talking to the Scots or fallen asleep straight after dinner. The only thing I always take time to do (yes, we pilgrims are pretty stressed most of the time) is to complete my hiking statistics for the day. Today is our 15th day and so far we have walked 313.5 km minus the cheated

7.5 km that we were driven near Estaing. That is a total of 321 km. We still have to walk 451 km before we get to the first stop in Spain called Roncesvalles and I just found out today that from there it is another 787 km to Santiago. That means that from here we must walk a total of 1238 km to Santiago. When I shouted that number out with joyful excitement René broke out in a fit of laughter. I leave you with that and send you my regards until the next travel update! Barbara.

PS: I'm only just beginning to leave real life behind and embrace our existence as vagabonds. I'm surprised how long it has taken to find distance from normal life because I was expecting that it would kick in as soon as we departed – kind of like the feeling we used to have when we came home and threw our schoolbags into a corner and were simply on summer holiday for two months. It isn't like that here. Somehow I feel like I'm *still* carrying my schoolbag.

Cahors, 8 October

In the morning everything always takes so long. As a pilgrim you don't really pack but instead you take

56

apart one household and move into a new one. You have to take the olive oil from the kitchen in a plastic coke bottle, the salt in a little aluminium box, the soap from the bathroom, the towel from the window sill, a t-shirt from the radiator, the shoe polish from the front room and the butter and cheese from the fridge. It takes about an hour to collect and stow everything in our backpacks which seem to be shrinking daily for some strange reason. But today we managed to leave by 8 o'clock and it was still quite dark outside. The nuns eat breakfast very early, so we decided to get up with the sound of the church bells at seven.

Of course the dreaded "Bois du Grezal" was in fact a sweet little oak forest. After all, thieves and robbers have acquired more inconspicuous appearances since the introduction of the *Code Civil*.

On our descent into Cahors which felt more like an airplane landing because it was so steep we sang children's songs and themes from children's television programmes – with many gaps in the lyrics. Walking obviously affects the brain in some way. Sometimes it stimulates our thoughts but when it's too much it has the same effect as alcohol. We have also noticed that we are speaking about childhood experiences more on our day trips. Even our dreams have focussed on childhood days, old apartments we used to live in and long-lost friends. Most of them are stories we have never told each other before, ones that we thought we had forgotten, just like so many other trivialities like my friend Siller's enormous tree house and that I once had to do my friend Severin's homework because he noticed that I had copied mine from Alfred Polgar. When do we ever have time to just let our thoughts wander completely aimlessly? It is precisely this wandering of thoughts or "free association" that is central to psychoanalysis and may contribute to the therapeutic effect the Way is said to have. Maybe pilgrimage is a form of "psychowalkalyisis".

Cahors suddenly appears behind a hilltop and like in a badly-dubbed film the noise of the town starts simultaneously – cars, trains, ambulance, fire engines form one loud honking and rushing. Cahors is the biggest city on the French part of the route. I had only heard of it because it was the origin of a certain wine, but this doesn't seem to make any sense now since there are only oak forests far and wide. And suburbs with tasteless villas whose main features are automatic garage doors and alarm systems. Suddenly we are inside Cahors, but we feel like we are on the outside. It is strange how much just 15 days of a different lifestyle have affected our perception. We walk past a school with a sign saying "Lycée". It is a hideous cement block with barbed wire around it. It reminds us of the kind of farmers who never let their animals out in the open. There are children running after a ball on the asphalt playground. Behind them are the fenced-off forests. It takes us a while to realise that most schools look like this. We must be going a little crazy, we think, and others must agree with us because we greet strangers we meet along the street. Even though we were raised in the city we have forgotten its rules. In the city one doesn't greet strangers and one doesn't look strangers in the eye for too long, especially not looking like we do.

Nevertheless, the city also has its benefits: namely launderettes with dryers. And great cafés. And elegant people (who make us feel rather uncomfortable in the state we are in). And bookstores. And many different newspapers. I devour the supplement of the *Süddeutsche Zeitung* about the Frankfurt Book Fair. I can't believe I'm in Cahors during the Frankfurt Book Fair!

We have permission to stay in the local youth hostel. The people there are very kind and helpful and put an extra bed into one of the rooms for us. Throughout our whole youth we never spent the night in a youth hostel, and now we are here. I suppose it's never too late for some things in life.

Lascabanes, 9 October

We went to a sports shop in the morning to buy new t-shirts. The shop assistant identified us as pilgrims straight away and tried to coax our motives out of us by saying: "Gosh, there are so many reasons why people go on pilgrimages…" This only made clear to us that we still didn't know what our reasons were. She went on to tell us about an acquaintance who was supposed to have his leg amputated. When it was saved, he kept his word and went to Santiago. Unfortunately we can't provide her with a similar story. So we say *"Prendre recul"*, which means to gain distance. With a little bit of distance you can see everything clearer and don't get caught up in the inanities of daily life, and so you have new ideas. Perhaps an overview prevents you from overlooking too many things.

We left Cahors via the impressive Pont Valentre, a medieval fortified bridge. We then climbed a slippery rise secured by iron hooks (the only dangerous part of our trip yet) and gained height very swiftly. Afterwards we walked along and under the motorway and along an asphalt road. When we finally reached the typical oak forest we were so used to, we were exhausted from our trip through civilisation and my knees had begun to hurt. "We can just hitchhike the last few kilometres," I said. And I kept saying it with every car that speeded past us – a sort of running gag if you will.

But then, so suddenly and unexpectedly that it almost scared us, someone stopped and got out of the car. He wore a red sweater with a tie underneath and his moustache reminded us a little of good old Marcello Mastroianni.

We asked him if he were driving to Lascabanes to which he responded with the grand gesture of shaking our hands. Yes, you guessed it right – a politician. He introduced himself: "I am the mayor of Lascabanes" and five minutes later we were in his kingdom. Lascabanes is a nice but dead little place and secretly we asked ourselves whom this mayor really ruled over.

Monsieur le maire is extremely proud of his newly built *gîte d'étape* – and rightly so. The old building next to the church has been converted into a 3-star pilgrim hostel with a long table in the dining room, a small coffee room in the reception hall, spacious rooms with en-suite showers and brand new beds that don't make you feel like you are sinking into nothingness. There is a large fully-equipped kitchen and a little shop where pilgrims can buy whatever they might need. We buy a tin of ravioli and so fulfil a childhood dream we rarely had granted because our mothers cooked too well. Ursula has also been here, six days ago and left a message in the book: "After two rough days and an even rougher night (I had to sleep in a barn in Pech Olli because the *gîte d'étape* was closed) I'm seriously enjoying this lovely accommodation. Thanks! Ursula (Hof/Bavaria -> Santiago.)"

Lauzarte, 10 October

Barbara, our centre for statistical analysis, has just calculated that we walk an average of 21.5 km a day and that therefore we would require 73 days to complete our journey. 18 days have passed so we have another 55 ahead of us. It would be nice if we could pick up our pace, but the weather forbids it. If we could have a nap in the sunshine after lunch every day it would be much easier to walk for longer, but for one it is too cold and for another the days are already becoming visibly shorter.

Due to the cold, we treated ourselves to lunch in a restaurant today, where we ate very well (which was surprising — and I say that without irony). It was a delicious omelette with porcinis. The restaurant was quite refined so we were a little embarrassed to leave little piles of dirt on the seats when we left.

The wind was irritating but the path was pretty

nonetheless. We saw many idyllic farms that reminded us of the nice little toy houses we used to place plastic cows, chickens and trees in front of when playing as children. The farms in Tarn-et-Garonne are similarly pretty and well-arranged as our playthings used to be.

Lauzerte is impressively positioned on the top of a hill. One could probably rebuild an entire model village with all the building material (partly still from the Renaissance) that is slowly deteriorating here. Lauzarte seems dead on first impression, but that is deceptive. There are many great restaurants and many young people and from about midnight onwards there is a real nightlife "scene". And if you are really lucky, like we were, you arrive on a Saturday and experience one of the wonderful jazz concerts in the café on the main square.

Saint-Antoine, 12. October

Meanwhile, two days have passed and we have dealt with our worst crisis yet. I'll start from the beginning: first a monsieur from Lauzarte urged us to avoid our route on the GR 65 to Moissac because there was a hunt for wild boar in the forest we would have to cross. Apparently the hunters shoot at anything that moves, including people dressed in yellow, red and blue like us.

So we walked along the main road, which was pretty severe. The cars racing past us not only scared us but the bad air gave us headaches. Fortunately after two hours a nice young man came to our rescue and gave us a ride to a less busy road which we then took to Moissac.

Moissac is a pretty place and even unreligious people should not miss out on viewing Saint-Pierre church and monastery. The frescos inside the church have been completely preserved, which makes it a rare and impressive experience. There is an enormous cedar tree in the courtyard of the monastery which has a beautiful effect on its surrounding by casting ever-changing shadows in the sunlight. This treasure was nearly torn down in the last century in order to make way for the railway.

After seeing the sites we went to the tourism

office or *"syndicat d'initiative"*. There we paid for the *gîte d'étape* and found out where the key to it was hidden. I will not reveal this hiding place here, because the *gîte d'étape* of Moissac is located outside the town next to a camping site and is by far the ugliest dump we have seen yet. Half of the lights don't work, the mattresses are so dirty you wouldn't want to put your sleeping bag let alone your body on them, the bathroom and toilets are in an appalling state and everything smells of a mixture of sewage and mould. We didn't shower because that way we knew we would stay cleaner without it. Besides, the shower had those plastic curtains that make me feel uncomfortable. I hate them. And they love me. I hate them, because they love everyone. They have mould stains and dirty edges and that's what they smell like too. And if I let my hypochondriac imagination go a little I can actually see the fungus growing on them. They sidle up to you shamelessly, incessantly flapping and if you don't pay attention in the shower for just one second, they stick to your whole body and you can't get rid of them.

66

We didn't see any other open hotels so we left our rucksacks in the room and walked all the way back into town to eat a pizza. On the way back it began to pour and we arrived in our quarters completely soaked. But we couldn't bring ourselves to lie down because we were so repulsed by everything, so we sat by the light of a naked bulb and wondered whether there weren't any more pleasant ways of spending time and money. After all neither of us considers the world to be completely miserable or a corrective institute but actually quite a likeable planet – so why suffer voluntarily? Why spend every day walking? Why get up tomorrow and put on damp clothes and walk to the next mouldy dump? The only thing that stopped us from going home that night was that although we had storage space for our furniture, we had no home for it.

Adding to our crisis was the fact that we didn't have any deeply religious motives for our pilgrimage and therefore obtain our identity as "pilgrims" from the outside. We are pilgrims because other people see us as that. But since Cahors no one has made us feel like pilgrims anymore. Instead we are treated more like irritating budget holidaymakers, which is essentially what we are.

There was nothing we could do, so in the end we lay down to sleep, very awkwardly and uncomfortably. It rained non-stop all night. We not only heard it but saw it with awful clarity in the streetlight that was positioned right outside our window.

When we stepped out in the morning, the sun was rising and shining in our faces. We decide to keep going. The Way of St James's magnetic effect is astonishing. I think it's almost impossible to give up once you have started walking. As if to confirm this, the path presents itself at its best. We walk along avenues of plane trees alongside the leisurely rolling Canal du Midi and the only thing interrupting this pleasurable walk is the nuclear power station in the distance. The steam clouds it is expelling seem to be anticipating mushroom clouds.

The landscape has changed dramatically. There are vineyards and fruit plantations as well as tomato and melon fields. The south is finally becoming really southern.

Arriving in Saint-Antoine also motivated us. It is a small town – the kind of place tourism guides would refer to as "picturesque". The population is predominantly British – every second house in the region is up for sale, but here nearly everything has been sold already.

We see a young lady sitting on a stone wall. Hat, walking stick, rucksack, hiking shoes – no doubt, a pilgrim. We approach her and introduce ourselves. Her name is Sophie and she left Le Puy a week before us but has had a slower journey because she injured herself on her very first day. The first time she swung her rucksack onto her back, she dislodged one of her ribs. This, admittedly, sounds like an entirely unscientific diagnosis, but apparently it hurts a lot. Since then she has slowly reduced the weight of her load from fourteen kilos to just five. Nonetheless, she still cries and screams a lot when she is walking. Today she is feeling fine though, so she wants to keep going for a little longer. We hope to meet her again in Lectoure tomorrow.

Our host, Madame Dupont, is an attractive older

woman with smiling eyes and a resolute walk. She gives us the keys to the small Romanic-Mozarabic church which in my opinion easily outdoes its opulent competitor in Moissac. Madame Dupont also provides us with a gas heater and cooks for us with care. This time we get six instead of four courses: soup, toast, salad, pastries, meat, cheese and dessert. We feel totally satisfied. It just feels wonderful to know that there is someone who isn't completely indifferent to how we are doing. It only makes sense to me now, why travelling salesmen and other people who travel a lot for work prefer quarters that have some sort of family touch.

Madame Dupont's guest book provides us with another pleasant surprise: "To all female pilgrims: beware of any dogs on your journey, I was gently nibbled by one on my bottom... And to all under-nourished pilgrims: Stuff yourselves with couscous and wash it down with a bottle of red wine. Thank you Saint-Antoine! Ultreïa, Ursula and Marco."

So the two have finally found each other; the down-to-earth German and the Swiss dreamer! Ursula seems pretty taken by Marco: I suppose we don't need to look any further into her comments about nibbled bottoms and red wine... But we are very excited to see what will become of them.

Lectoure, 13 October

Today is the very first full day that it has been sunny and wind-free since we left Le Puy three weeks ago. I read something about an Azores high in *Sud-Ouest*, the only newspaper that is usually available around here. In this weather everything is suddenly so different. I'm beginning to understand why the weather is always a top subject, even though it really only has existential meaning for farmers (and pilgrims).

The path is comfortably leading us between fields and hills, past castles and forests and brings us new acquaintances. We spot a couple riding towards us and can tell they are English from more than 100 m away due to their flawless clothing and posture – her on a horse, him on a donkey...

Sometimes the path becomes too comfortable for our liking. We can see on our map that it is going in a zigzag line all the way to Lectoure passing every chapel and church in the surrounding area along the way, which is nice because they can be very pretty and are normally situated next to ancient pagan mineral spring sanctuaries. But today we just don't feel like this kind of winding route and decide to take an ingenious shortcut. The only problem is that in the exact place where we want to skip out on a large bend of the path there is a large sign reading: "Private path. No trespassing. Beware – Pit-bull terrier." We are pretty sure that the pit-bull part is made up, but somehow don't feel the need to go and find out.

Lectoure is somewhat mediocre in its appeal. It has an impressive cathedral, but it isn't particularly inviting. The *gîte d'étape* is all right, located in an old frame house. Sophie is nowhere to be found and we wonder where she might be.

La Romieu, 14 October

La Romieu is a small and charming place where Arnaud d'Aux was born around 1260 and later, as a cardinal became one of Pope Clement V's most influential advisors. That is why this town has such a large church and an impressive early gothic monastery. Everything here seems to shout: "I have history", even the *gîte d'étape*. It has been somewhat clumsily but originally integrated into a former church from the 12th century.

One could really imagine what the summer must be like today: absolute calm in the air, blue sky, peaceful views. When we arrived in La Romieu we spent a whole two hours in shorts and t-shirts sitting in a café in the sunshine on the main square quenching our thirst with a "Pression", watching the cats doze and the dogs yawning. It was wonderful. But I'm sure if it were actually summer we wouldn't have been half as relaxed, seeing as we may not have found a bed with so many pilgrims around. We have heard many stories along the way about veritable races to hostels, fights over hostel beds, hot water in the shower and use of kitchen facilities during peak season from June to August. The only thing we have found here is Sophie, which made us very happy. She has, in the meantime, swapped her backpack for a ribcage-friendly shoulder bag and as a result looks a bit like an overgrown schoolgirl.

We spent all evening cooking and eating and drinking and talking with her. We still haven't dared ask her directly why she is walking the route, but instead we have discussed how difficult the "re-socialisation" process will be after our pilgrimage. It already seems very strange to imagine going into a house and not washing our socks and t-shirts and then drying them on the radiator. And in the real world it isn't normal to use any stretch along the road as a public toilet. We also need to learn that it isn't really normal to cut pieces off any rope you find lying around "just in case" you might need it as a washing line. And when you have sugar in a café or bar, you can just leave the rest there when you are finished with it. Just as you can't really go into strangers' gardens and steal their herbs in order to make tea or – like today – spaghetti with butter and sage.

Condom, 15 October
Dear Michi!
As usual we are sitting in a little bar drinking tea and Armagnac. In the background they are showing

"Falco the Detective" on television, which is making us a little homesick here in this little town with such a strange name. Yes, it really is called Condom and has a very large dome that dominates the centre along with several Armagnac cellars which are very worth seeing. What made me far more excited than Condom today was the fact that we glimpsed an enormous mountain range glowing in the distance beyond the hills today: The Pyrenees! They are still very far away, but we are very excited about reaching them soon.

We still share the strange feeling of being nomads with the other pilgrims we meet. This means we not only share many experiences but also a toilet and a shower and a kitchen. It also means strangers quickly turn into what can nearly be described as family members.

One example of this would be Sophie, with whom we spent last evening and this evening too. She seems very cheerful, is 33 years old, smokes cigarettes without filters, is an editor for various publications and is very charming. She had a strange accident on her first day where she "dislocated" a rib through just one clumsy movement. It seems like walking the Way means you always have to expect the worst. Sophie said: "Whenever you think everything is going all right, something happens where you need help from someone, are in danger or are uncomfortable in some way." As a pilgrim, you put yourself into a self-created situation of difficulty which is sometimes so difficult you can't get out of it on your own.

The same thing happened to me today. Usually I have some pain in either my hip or my knee and today, for the first time, I thought it had finally gone away for the first time. It was my first truly carefree day! But about ten minutes later I tripped into a pothole and sprained my ankle so badly that it swelled up to the size of a tennis ball, leaving me to limp the rest of the way. Isn't that peculiar? I've heard similar accounts from many other pilgrims. The route seems not to permit anyone to just walk for fun. Many begin as mere tourists, but all of them end as pilgrims.

Due to my misfortune we ended up not only meeting Henri and Vélimir, but also Sophie and three "new" pilgrims – all of which happened in an ugly hospital-like dormitory. I'm very curious how things will continue tomorrow, but most of all I am concerned about my ankle. At the moment, every step is painful, but I won't worry about it now. If I have learned one thing these past few weeks, it's that there is no use in planning too far ahead, because nothing turns out as expected anyway. If I hadn't hurt myself today, we could have walked much further than 16 km and as a result would have ended in a different village. But then we wouldn't have found Sophie again. The glass is always half-full as a pilgrim, which is really your only choice. I have noticed that I have become very fatalistic on this trip. The idea that there is some sort of reasoning behind every event keeps creeping up on us; the only problem is that we can't figure out what that reasoning might be.

On a totally different note: we have been walking behind a Swiss man for the past few days who is travelling the Way of St James with his donkey. According to the "pilgrim's mail" he must be about two days ahead of us. So instead of following the signs now, we follow the donkey's little hoof prints. "Look, the donkey!" we shout like happy children whenever we discover one of his prints in the mud. Somehow we don't feel silly at all at the thought of following a donkey somewhere.

But now I have to hobble after my husband. I think he is desperate to go to sleep! Lots of love, Barbara.

Le Haget, 16 October

One extra note on Condom: Ursula and Marco were there! We finally found another of their clues – and what a clue it was! "Today we aren't writing about food for once (even though it was very good). Life as a pilgrim can have some serious disadvantages. If you are walking together with someone you begin to exchange vices. I have started smoking and Marco now drinks red wine. Let's see if we ever make it to Santiago. The gîte is great and the showers are nearly perfect. Thanks! Ursula.

That's pretty cheeky... I make the first pizza of my life, it is actually edible and Ursula doesn't want to talk about the food! I wonder if she really liked it as much as she said. We want to say thank you for the clean, large, comfortable, noble, beautiful, good, practical, nice-smelling, modern, hospitable, quiet, bright, smoker-friendly, close-to-town, well-positioned, colourful hostel and also for the hammocks. Marco." (By hammock, Marco means the beds and I can only interpret the rest of his adjectives as pure irony.)

In the morning Barbara can hardly walk. What to do? We certainly don't want to stay in Condom, because the hostel is so shoddy but walking a full stretch will be impossible. But there are buses in Condom that are going in the right direction. We hide in our seats and turn our heads away from the window so that our colleagues don't see us driving by. Funnily enough, the woman selling us the bus tickets points out that it was *"classique"* to sustain an injury before Condom and then take the bus to Eauze.

I'm sure we missed a great deal of the route on the bus. It is also kind of bizarre to make an entire day's journey in just one hour by bus. But the last stretch from Eauze to Le Haget was just bearable for

Barbara's ankle. The swelling actually went down a little as she walked. However, she had to be very careful not to sprain it again since the farmers plough through the path which runs along the edge of their corn field, which can make it very difficult to walk smoothly. Départements Gers and Landes are characterised by extensive agricultural development: there are enormous corn fields that are only used to feed the millions of geese and ducks to make paté – the most famous product of the "Sud-Ouest".

Fortunately there are a few small farmers left who prevent the scenery from becoming all too monotonous and provide us with the company of some animals. Using bits of old bread and cheese rind that we always carry with us we have made many new "friends" among them: three horses, one donkey, one cat, one lizard and two dogs. The latter belong to Le Haget, a small farm whose owner also runs a small pilgrim hostel. Xavier, the fully-bearded, charming host gave us a sleeping area right next to the stable and the shower is actually in the stables opposite. Everything here is Spartan but we feel very comfortable. The farm is well taken care of and pretty. A cedar-lined avenue leads up to its old stone walls and the dogs come running up to greet you. Xavier receives us with two glasses of beer. When he notices our confused look, he just laughs and says "Enjoy it and don't look so scared. Your stay won't be more expensive because of the drinks!" We do as we are told and truly enjoy our beers. We then decide to meet back in the main house for dinner at 8 o'clock.

Xavier welcomes us with beer, olives and sausage to tide us over before "the starter is ready". His wife is there too but remains in the background. She is a teacher and doesn't involve herself with the care of the pilgrims too much. "That's Xavier's hobby," she points out. "Yes, it is really just a hobby," he shouts from the kitchen. "After all, not many pilgrims pass by here anyway. And I bet there will be even less after the dreaded year 2000. But I'm interested in people. I like talking to them. And that is why I run this little hostel. Most pilgrims are extraordinary people. Although I have to add there are surprisingly many crazy people among them too." He tells us the town used to be called Hôpital and there was a large pilgrim hospice of the Order of the Holy Grave and he was now trying to continue this tradition with modest means. Xavier knows the route very well and makes fun of those people trying to walk the "real" historical path: "The historic path is a farce. There are seven proven historical paths alone in the stretch between the Sainte Christie chapel around the corner and the main road 150 m away. The right path has nothing to do with geography. The Way of St James is made by those people walking it."

There is an open grand piano standing in the living room with music on it. To perfect this image, the dog has positioned itself beautifully underneath it. On the sofa next to it there is an acoustic guitar. I enquire whether the family plays a lot. "Oh, I play very badly," says Xavier. "But I come from a musical family. You are from the land of the operetta. You must know the composer Jacques Offenbach then?" We nod. "Well, Offenbach was my great grandfather's biggest rival in Paris at the end of last century. My grandfather was Salieri and Offenbach was Mozart, so to speak…"

We then sit down to eat at the massive wooden dining table. Xavier serves us soup, then fried quail with potato gratin followed by salad, cheese and raspberry cake. We drink two bottles of wine and through the course of the evening become friends. It is long past midnight when we return to the stables and sleep fantastically. The next day, after breakfast we would have stayed for another few hours, chatting together, if the route hadn't drawn us back in.

Aire-sur-l'Adour, 17 October

The day was sunny and the path runs beautifully between fields and forests. There is a stream that needs to be crossed shortly after Le Haget. After the smaller bridge, the correct path leads straight ahead through a cornfield. We followed the trodden path along the river which was also very nice. The fact that it "cost" us an hour doesn't bother us that much anymore, having been on the road for three weeks. We have learned not to get angry about things that can't be changed anymore. Moreover, it has often been the case that supposed mishaps ended up being particularly lucky experiences.

In Nogaro we spend one coffee thinking how to continue our journey. The next town with a hostel, Aire-sur-l'Adour, is 33 km away and even with healthy legs that would be a great distance for one afternoon. Added to that, Barbara is still in pain from her ankle injury. But we also don't want to stay in Nogaro – we want to keep going! So, we decide to continue without a plan.

This turns out to be very successful until we see an ominous patch of dark clouds coming towards us from the west near Luppé. We can feel the air getting heavy and know it will soon rain. We are a bit down because we would so much have loved to make it to the Adour… We decide to walk to the main road and have a look at the hotel available in Luppé. Although it has one star more than our budget allows we decide we have no choice because it is already beginning to rain. When we get to the main road we can't figure out in which direction to head, and the drops are already hitting down on us. We cross the street to get a better view and in that moment a car stops next to us. A woman gets out and drops her bottles off at the glass recycling. "Do you happen to be going to Aire-sur-l'Adour?" And ten minutes later we are there. (If we hadn't taken the wrong path this morning, then we wouldn't have been here at this moment and would never have met the kind lady who gave us a lift – a suitable example for the way that detours can sometimes turn out to be shortcuts…) And best of all we don't feel as guilty with this type of cheating as we did taking the bus yesterday. I suppose it's kind of like the difference between murderous robbery and manslaughter out of self-defence.

When we arrive in Aire-sur-l'Adour in the pouring rain we still have quite a way to go since the hostel is in the *"centre de loisirs"* slightly outside of the town. We get there, completely soaked, and everything is closed. We dial the phone numbers in our guides – nothing. Luckily we had taken the number of a woman with available rooms when we were in Condom. Fifteen minutes later Aline Porte picks us up at the phone booth. She is a portly, cheerful woman and her old red 2 CV suits her perfectly. "We always pick up our pilgrims" she explains, "because our farm isn't just a little outside of town but also quite a bit upwards of it…"

Soon after, we move into our nice little room. "Bring me your laundry," says Madame Porte, "I'll wash it in the machine, and if we hang it above the stove it will be dry and ready tomorrow morning."

We have our dinner with the entire family (three generations). I don't think they really notice us – as if we were just two more large children at the table. It is a real feast: vegetable soup, roast duck, cake, and red wine. The family lives predominantly from rearing poultry. We learn a lot about ducks, geese and French agriculture and they find out a lot about Austria and pilgrims. We feel very comfortable in this warm atmosphere. Around midnight we go to bed and fall asleep satisfied.

Arzaq-Arraziguet, 18 October

The Porte family was very kind to us the next morning
as well. Initially we had agreed that the price for the
room, dinner and breakfast was 300 Francs for the
pair of us but in the morning Mrs Porte wanted no
such sum. She would accept no more than 200 Francs
and insisted on also giving us a jar of "Rilettes de
canard", a type of pâté. We have already been told
several times that these gestures should simply be
accepted with a smile and a thank-you. It is insulting
to still attempt to pay more if hosts offer less. The
best way to show your gratitude is to send a postcard
from Santiago or a gift from your own home town
upon your return.

Madame Porte's daughter drove us back to the path
in her car and said, "I'll drive you a little further along
the way. You won't see much but cornfields today, so
you needn't worry about missing anything."

So we ended up missing Aire-sur-l'Adour, the
former capital of Alarich II's western Gothic empire
where one can still see Roman-pagan, Gothic-Arian
and Christian culture living side by side. Instead we

met someone new. The timing was perfect. We had only been walking for half an hour when an odd couple came trotting toward us. It was the Swiss pilgrim and his donkey! Jean says he is lost because he can't find his way through all the cornfields. Jean is a retired mechanic from Geneva. He departed from there in late August and is taking it slowly. Sometimes things take longer because his donkey needs taking care of. He had already spent one week waiting to get new horseshoes. Jean likes walking and is taking the trip for a Swiss charity that helps the elderly. He is being sponsored by several companies and once he reaches Santiago with his donkey Modestine he will receive the sums and pass them on to the charity.

As we continue on with Jean and Modestine I am reminded of one of my favourite sentences from Kurt Tucholsky's *A Pyrenees Book*: "It dripped down from the sky and the donkeys, the leader and I, this is not an apposition, were already wet when we left the village behind us." At first we are quite envious of Jean. Modestine carries his entire luggage and he can walk freely. Soon, however, this envy turns into sympathy. Not because of the apposition but because of the opposition he faces.

We suspected it when we caught site of them for the first time – they were both equally covered in mud and even smelled similar. It's no wonder, really, because they are always together day and night. And they have to be. Since Modestine needs to graze at night, Jean usually camps right next to her. Consequently he rarely spends the night in a hostel and cannot shower very often. What is worse for him is that he hardly meets any people that way. Although he doesn't talk that much, we can tell he is very happy for our company.

The good thing is that we were also useful to him at a difficult point on the route. Modestine, you must know, refuses to cross narrow bridges. And she is afraid of water. As a result, we were stuck at the edge of a tiny brook with only a tiny bridge crossing it. Neither sweet talking nor hits with a walking stick had any effect whatsoever. She didn't move an inch. One might think that three adults could move a small donkey effortlessly but that is very much incorrect.

Jean had already explained in Le Haget that: "Donkeys are extremely strong. As opposed to humans, they think before they act and if they come to the conclusion that they don't want to do something because it isn't sensible, then they simply will not do it."

And so it was. So we had to trick her.

We tied a rope around her legs and tried to make her fall forwards. When faced with the choice of toppling or crossing through the water, she decided to walk. The only problem was that this happened so quickly that Jean landed in the stream and we were soaked from head to toe.

In contrast, our lunch break was perfectly idyllic the small church of Sensacq. Since it was raining once again, the three of us sat inside eating cheese sandwiches and the donkey grazed off the top of the graves outside.

In the afternoon, when the pilgrim normally begins to slow down just a little, Modestine really got going, so we had to keep up. I doubt we have ever been as fast as on that afternoon. Hence we hardly had time to think about the little sign we passed on the front of a house that read "Compostelle 924 km". Jean got so excited by this that he did a small victory dance and laughed out loud. "See! We are getting somewhere! Isn't it amazing how quick we are! Hardly anything left to go!" When he saw the bewildered looks on our faces he quietly mumbled "Well you know, just 924 km left…"

In Arzacq-Arraziguet there are only 919 km left until Santiago. The town seems dead – typical for a Sunday afternoon. Once again we feel like we are "outside" and everyone else is "inside" – in cars, in a garden, in a home, in a family… Jean finds a place in the camping site next to our *gîte d'étape*. We convince him to leave Modestine on her own for a while and come and eat a pizza with us. It is his first meal with other people in two weeks and he has tears in his eyes.

Arthez-de-Béarn, 19 October
We leave Jean and Modestine in the morning because it will take far too long for him to take down his tent and pack up the donkey. "You'll catch up with us

anyway" we say and wave to them as we depart. We never see them again. But we have also lost Sophie and Henri and Vélimir and Guy-Marie and Véronique. As a pilgrim, one learns never to make a big fuss over goodbyes, just like one never sets meeting points for the evening. Everyone knows that day journeys often end very differently than one has planned.

We do, however, find news from our faceless friends Ursula and Marco. After a sunny and pleasant day that led us over smooth hills and through ochre coloured fields we arrive tired in Arthez. We stop for a beer in a café in the square and try to find out where the *gîte d'étape* is. The lady in charge of it lives directly opposite. She accompanies us, unlocks the doors and shows us to our room. Barbara looks in the guest book to see if she recognises any names but there is no trace of Ursula and Marco. Our hostess comments "Not many people travel at this time of year, but a few days ago there were two pilgrims here. I haven't laughed like that for a long time. One was German and the other Italian." We ask if the Italian could have been Swiss. "It's possible," she says, "but who knows anything about the Swiss anyway. But he was a handsome boy, that's for sure." No doubt – that was Marco. Indiscreetly, we persist and ask whether the couple seemed like they were a little in love. She bursts out laughing "A little!? They were like two lovebirds!"

Navarrenx, 20 October

Our host's son reveals a shortcut to us. Instead of the route, we are supposed to follow the GR 65 and walk down toward Mont. "Then you pass my factory," he said and meant the enormous "elf"-plant in which the local natural gas supplies are processed. After the factory we are to turn right and cross the river on a former pipeline. The whole thing sounds a little scary, which isn't helped by the fact that we can hardly understand the young man who speaks in a strong Béarn dialect which is only distantly related to French.

To our great relief, the pipeline leads over a bridge. The bridge heads are however covered with barbed wire and warning signs with sculls on them.

Fortunately we find the hole in the fence just where we were told and climb over the bridge. At the other end, the situation is similar but again we find the hole in the fence and soon after we are back on the Way. Fortunately, this shortcut didn't cost us any time at all. I suppose the young man just wanted to show us "his factory" because he is proud of it.

After the gas factory we only met three new people, including a friendly farmer who told us about the region's history. Béarn was only united with the French kingdom in 1620. Before that it was once independent, once Protestant, once Spanish and once subject to British influence.

The other two people we met were also farmers who happened to meet at a crossroads with their tractors. Since we were just having a break there, we watched them chatting for a good half hour without getting off their tractors or even switching the engines off.

From our little resting spot we had an – and I say this without wanting to overuse the expression – unforgettable view of the Pyrenees. I think we could almost see the entire length of the mountain range, the jagged, reddish, high peaks in the east and the softer, rounder tips in the west. Again I was reminded of Tucholsky's wonderful *A Pyrenees Book* which really should be called "The Pyrenees Book". On the first page he reminisces about geography lessons in school: "Pyrenees – that was the rusty brown thing on a predominantly green and black map. In it were some dotted mountains and on the right and left hand side was blue, where they dipped into the sea … Oh and they separated Spain and France. And one always had to think just a little more carefully when spelling the name."

I still have to think quite carefully every time I write the word.

The weather is wonderful, our goal – the Pyrenees– is in sight, which is highly motivating, but today's stretch is extremely tiring due to the many ups and downs of the route. We only arrive in Navarrenx as it is getting dark, too late for the priest's daily pilgrim reception. According to the rumours we have heard, he is a very unconventional and upbeat person. The *gîte d'étape* is located in the town's former arsenal and we can't find any flaws in it. We discover a message in the guest book that irritates us. "Although I slept alone, it was very nice. No wonder – the hostess told me exactly which mattress was the best! Ursula (Hof/ Bayern -> Santiago) PS. I would never have thought it, but you can still get blisters after 2000 km. Unbelievable!" Where is Marco? Is Ursula suffering so much that she is even getting blisters?

Saint-Palais, 21 October

Basque country begins right behind Navarrenx. One doesn't hear much good about the Basques in the papers or on television, but the French Basques are clearly less radical than the Spanish. This is because they would hardly benefit from independence since the only source of income in their country is rearing sheep and pigs. For the Spanish however, it is very different. As with many other European countries, the north is the centre of industry. So as expected, the conflict is not just about patriotism but about money, which the Spanish Basques would rather share with their few French brothers than with the entire

Spanish nation... One doesn't really speak of this openly in France and luckily I won't be tempted to in Spain because I speak neither Basque nor Spanish. Other than a few walls covered with graffiti we don't really notice anything radical on either side anyway. Moreover, the Basque region is very large and the terror centres are somewhere else. We were reminded of a Peruvian musician whom we met at a music festival in Graz. He was extremely relieved about the fact that Austria wasn't really as bad as he had expected. When we asked what could possibly be that bad here he just whispered: "The mafia!" Before he had left Peru, he had studied a map of the world and his wife had almost refused to let him go because Graz was so close to Sicily – and Sicily was said to be a dangerous place.

We have an utterly pleasant impression of Basque Country: the sun is shining, the people are very friendly and everyone greets you along the way. The names of the towns are written in both French and Basque on the signs, but in the towns themselves we cannot recognise the shops because they are only in

Basque. The language contains many As and Zs and sounds entirely foreign to us.

The landscape has hardly changed. The woods smell enticingly of autumn and the cows in the fields are called "Blondes d'Acquitaine" which suits their noble look very well. The only thing different is the water which flows stronger and is cleaner. Many streams lead down to this plateau which makes us feel very happy but also worried for Jean and Modestine.

Saint-Palais, our destination for today, is positioned some distance away from the path. We have heard many good reports about this Franciscan monastery and they are all true. Although the sleeping room is very simple, the welcome we receive from the monks (there are only three left) is particularly warm. Two-thirds of the monks are pretty old. They wear traditional brown wool habits and are barefoot in sandals. It seems their feet are entirely calloused. Hopefully that is enough to protect them from the cold.

We have dinner with them and five agricultural students, who are also living in the monastery. As with all other pious locations we have stayed, the food is good, conversation is merry and sleep is peaceful.

Ostabat, 22 October

We wake up in Saint-Palais to the sound of the monks singing. The echo of their prayers is so affecting that it feels as though the monks have multiplied overnight. But when we get to breakfast there are still only three of them. The youngest, who also seems to be in charge, writes the Franciscan motto *pax et bonum* into our pilgrim's pass in Basque: "*Bakea eta zeriona*" it reads, if I haven't misread his handwriting. We then have a short theological conversation about fate and determinism. Many pilgrims tell the monks about strange coincidences and begin to believe in the occurrence of a mysterious power that causes them. He however is sceptical of this interpretation. Would God really show himself to the world that directly? He thinks that some pilgrims are so guided by fate that they are prepared to turn any coincidence into a miracle.

He takes our 200 Francs after we have assured

him that we really aren't needy and can afford to pay for food and shelter – "after all you are an author" he notes. He recommends a visit to the little Museum of Saint-Palais. It is located right next to the town hall and tells us about the history of the Navarro region and the four major pilgrim routes. It is rather informative. One can, for instance, see a hollowed-out pumpkin shell that was used by most pilgrims as a water bottle. (Today, most people use lightweight aluminium flasks.) The museum also shows various symbols of Basque culture – stylised crosses, starbursts, pentagrams. The signs are still attached to tombstones or road signs today. No wonder the Basques have so much trouble. All cultures that haven't yet unlearnt magic have difficulties fitting in.

Today's stretch to Ostabat is 11 km. At home we would consider that a Sunday walk to be proud of. Here, it is a day of rest.

In Hiriburia we spot a Basque crossroad sign called Gibraltar. (Gibraltar, in this case, has nothing to do with the straits but is a version of Salvatore.)

This is the point where the Ways of St James from Le Puy, Vézelay and Tours merge. The fourth traditional route from Arles will probably only link up with us near Puente La Reina.

Ostabat is a pleasant and sleepy village. When you sit in the first (and only) café on the square and watch the pigs sleeping, the cows grazing and the Pyrenees glowing, you are filled with a deep sense of peace. It is hard to believe that Ostabat was one of the most important pilgrim stops in the Middle Ages and that its hospices were once capable of holding up to 5000 people. The old house named "Ospitalia" that is now the *gîte d'étape*, is only a small reminder of that time. We feel very comfortable here. The neighbour in charge of the hostel brings us wood for the oven and gives us eggs for dinner. The people here are monosyllabic but very warm.

Saint-Jean-Pied-de-Port, 23 October
After one month of travelling we have now arrived at the foot of the Pyrenees. Tomorrow we will plunge into a new world. We are terribly excited about this

even though we have little experience of Spain and hardly speak the language.

Today it was really hot. The cause of this mysterious climate is a föhn storm which we know very well from the Alps. The educated French call it *"Le Foen"* and the others call it by its traditional name *"le fou"* or "the crazy one". The strong southern wind has also charmed the snakes out of hiding. We suddenly spot a viper on our path. It is very short, but wider than any I have ever seen before. We freeze in our tracks. It pauses, deciding whether to attack or not and finally it retreats. For the rest of the day, the sound of anything in the grass makes my skin crawl.

When we walk through St James's Gates at Saint-Jean-Pied-de-Port we feel quite proud of our achievement. We have walked more than 700 km already. Halftime.

We pick up our *"post restante"* at the post office (among it the travel guides for Spain which we sent ourselves), do some shopping and move into the ugly hostel. Then we look for Madame Débril, who is a legend on the route. We have heard more than once that if you go to Saint-Jean-Pied-de-Port, you have to visit Madame Débril. She will give us the *"Credencial de Peregrino"* the pilgrim pass that is required in Spain for staying in official pilgrim hostels or *"refugios"*. (We have also heard that there is a flourishing black market for fake passes in Saint-Jean-Pied-de-Port.) Our Canadian friends from earlier also told us about Madame Debril. They even forgave her for sending them on their way across the Pyrenees at three in the afternoon. Because of it, Guy-Marie and Veronique only arrived in Roncesvalles at eleven that night, having lost themselves in the fog and darkness along the way. They were so exhausted from this experience that the only managed to travel 5 km the next day. "But Madame Débril – you really must meet her." I will cut it short, well, shorter at least than our visit with the old lady who holds court and gives long speeches in her chaotic study. An older man was already sitting with her, looking suspiciously close to having a nervous breakdown. He repeatedly made references to his pilgrim pass and that the shops were about to close but it was hopeless. Madame Débril went on ranting about the poor quality of hiking guides, the pilgrims who dare stay in pilgrim hostels even though they have arrived here by train and about robbers who stole official rubber stamps from her office and about Antonio Gaudi's hideous palace in Astorga and about the "barbaric Basques" and and and... We waited exactly one and a half hours for her to finish. And the punchline at the end: it was all a complete waste of time because we already had all the necessary stamps to get our *Crendicial* in Roncesvalles. Madame Débril said she would prefer it that way because otherwise it would take up too much of her time. We spent the evening reading through all of our mail. It really makes you feel like home to receive long letters from friends. And we've been missing so much! And how well they have all been without us! It's almost infuriating!

Roncesvalles, 24 October

The Pyrenees are tricky. And that is not because they are particularly dangerous or exciting. In fact they are more like "cow hills" as the locals prefer to describe them. But they are still tricky, because you spend all day climbing them on a downhill slope and when you finally think the path will really go down hill the dramatic ascent to the Ibañeta pass begins.

We were advised not to take the old "Route Napoleon" because despite its beauty it can be very lonely. Since the weather was about to turn we were told to walk along the road. Walking along roads is rarely pleasurable, but is made even worse on this grey day by the Föhn storm that is blowing straight at us with a speed of 100 km/h and 0 per cent humidity.

Roncesvalles is peculiar. It consists of a monastery and two guest houses, which, as far as we can understand, also belong to the monks. Roncesvalles is much like a fortress: dark, cold, imposing and made of stone. The monastery was built by the bishop of Pamplona in 1132 because he felt sorry for all the pilgrims who either froze to death and/or were eaten by wolves. In the middle ages pilgrims were allowed to stay in Roncevalles for three days. They received food, drink, shelter, a bathroom and if they died anyway, a Christian burial. A large pilgrim grave was found near the cloister and legend has it that Roland, nephew of Charlemagne, who was beaten by the Basques in 778, is also buried there. However, there now are historians who dispute whether Charlemagne ever existed, let alone his nephew Roland. This just goes to show that many of the things educated people tell you along the route may just be stories rather than history.

Today, Roncesvalles has nearly as many pilgrims as during the medieval heyday of the Camino de Santiago. As if to underline this, our reception by a Kafkaesque official in the hostel is particularly impersonal. He bids us into his office. We are to take a seat at a suitable distance opposite his desk. He gives us a stern look and carefully checks our French stamp collection. Will he be able to tell that we took the bus once? No, he doesn't notice. We receive our *Credencial* after each giving our name, date of birth and profession. Then the austere man tries to explain something to us in Spanish. Unfortunately we don't understand him at all. Then he points to the clock and makes gestures which make it clear that we need to be in the *refugio* by ten in the evening because that is when it closes. And we need to leave by eight in the morning. Okay? Okay. So that's how it is here…

In the freezing-cold mattress room we see Charles again, the old French man whom we first met at Madame Débril's. He convinces us to go to mass with him since it is, after all, a tradition in Roncesvalles. He adds that he so wishes to have the pilgrim's blessing one receives from the priest. Bernard, a second French man, agrees with this. So we are confronted with Spanish Catholicism on our very first day in the country. Every last seat in the church is filled, there are blaring songs, colourful gowns, big gestures, naturalistic Jesus statues with lots of blood and oversized nails, incense, gold and silver and ornately decorated interiors. All of this can be slightly demanding for someone raised as a Protestant. And what is worse, our French friends bring us into a terribly awkward situation. At the end of mass, the priest asks the pilgrims to come to the altar, in Spanish and then in English. Since both of our new friends speak neither

107

of these languages (or any other foreign language for that matter), we have to point them in the right direction... and are stuck with them. Within seconds I am in a situation I couldn't even have imagined until recently: I am kneeling in front of a Spanish priest, who chants above me in Arabic-sounding English: "Gohooo wis Gohoood and prrray for us in Compostelle."

But the stress isn't over yet. Even though we are supposed to be at the hostel at ten, dinner is only served at nine. So we have to stuff ourselves and rush through the meal. Somehow, we still manage a short conversation with Charles. He is from Normandy and only walking toward Santiago for ten days. And Bernard is currently already on his third journey along the route. He is a strange old man, about 50 years old, and a media and PR consultant for large firms. At the moment he is writing a book about the "Angels of the Cabbala" which are apparently abundant along the route. We ask him for some more precise detail but he either doesn't want to or can't give them to us. Bernard went on his first trip to Santiago because of a bet. When drunk he had made a bet with his friends that he could get from Paris to Santiago without any money, which he did. He left with 500 Francs and returned with 300 Francs and the round trip took him only 14 days, getting the most support on his hitch-hiking pilgrimage from Portuguese truckdrivers.

In Roncesvalles, where everyone has to pass through, we finally find news from Ursula and Marco. One day before Ursula, Marco writes: "That was a super stint, wasn't it? It's harsh but absolutely beautiful to arrive here. And the landscape in the Pyrenees was also not bad. Marco (Ultreïa, Ursula)." Ursula's comment a day later is similarly indifferent: "After a wonderful day so close to the sky I have finally arrived here. I truly enjoyed the autumn sun but am now freezing even more. Greetings to all other pilgrims staying here! Ursula (Hof/Bayern -> Santiago)." Something must have happened between those two. Marco is obviously trying to play it cool. No more *pax et bonum*. Instead he writes "super" and "not bad". And he only left a standard pilgrim greeting "Ultreïa" for Ursula, and in brackets at that.

Pamplona, 25 October

What follows a föhn storm? A sudden temperature drop, of course. And Spain is no exception. This morning the rain is pouring down from the sky. We leave the *refugio* before eight, because after all, we are good pilgrims. The problem with this, however, is that neither of the two restaurants is open. Since there isn't a kitchen in the hostel either, we have to start walking without any breakfast in us.

After half an hour we are soaked to the bone. We stop in Burguete for a *"café con leche por favor"* to console us – luckily the coffee in Spain is delicious. We head back out into the rain again and slip and slide down the muddy forest floor. We are still worn out from yesterday's long stint and our hips feel kind of like they haven't been oiled properly. We pull into a bar in Espinal completely exhausted. The bar woman tells us that the village has no hotel but that she can call us a taxi to take us to the next town. We deliberate. Can we really begin the Spanish leg of the trip with a taxi ride? Things get worse. When we get into the taxi and are discussing the price of the journey,

110

the driver offers us a special discount for Pamplona. Driving 15 or 30 km doesn't really make a difference to him he explains, adding that the suburbs of Pamplona really aren't anything to write home about and that he knew a hotel in the main square where pilgrims got a discount.

A while later we check into the hotel La Perla with no regrets. The only thing that saddens us just a little is that we saw the transition from green wooded mountains to ochre plains in fast-forward rather than slow motion. Where we are now looks almost like desert to the northern European eye. Nonetheless we are delighted to have time to see Pamplona. The city is imperial, broadly structured but not cold and full of Mediterranean liveliness. It is the capital of the Navarra province (and formerly of the empire) and has about 200,000 inhabitants, making it the biggest city we have seen for a long time. This is probably the reason why we enjoy walking the streets from café to café so much, and marvel at the many elegant men and women we see.

Pamplona, which was dearly loved by Hemingway,

is the city in which bulls are let loose every year in July. The animals then chase through the narrow streets of the old city and hobby-toreros try to touch their horns because this is the ultimate test of manliness. From what we can tell, this spectacle is now afforded less importance than it used to. "It's just childishness provided for American tourists," says a bartender who fortunately speaks French. "And besides, there are so many people who come to the Sanfermines parties now that it is becoming more and more dangerous. There are people injured every year and even fatalities."

But when the bulls aren't charging through the small streets, one can really live nicely here. Everything caters to the outside world, for a life in the streets in which sociability is promoted, even in late October. The temperature is around 12 degrees, it is raining, and yet the tables in the arcades are all occupied.

We are uncomfortably conspicuous in this elegant and urbane setting due to our hiking gear which consists of dirty trousers, multicoloured rain jackets and the horrible combination of socks in espadrilles.

We look like complete aliens in this city and particularly in this fashionable café that is made entirely of brass, copper and marble and still manages to create a warm atmosphere.

As we study the passers-by, we notice two things: first, all Spanish people smoke. The only exceptions to this rule are children under the age of twelve. Secondly, everyone has bags under his/her eyes – much like Placido Domingo and Jose Carreras. Maybe it is because in this country, life takes place largely at night. This afternoon I thought Pamplona was a lively place. Now, at ten in the evening, it is really lively – about as lively as the City Festival in Vienna. It seems like every day here is somewhat of a festival. The amount of noise is certainly at a similar level. People practically sit on each others laps when telling stories. And the volume at which they do so makes it sound as if they are recounting the most exciting adventure of their lives.

In any case, we enjoy our little break from the holidays. We take the bus as far as the Pelote Stadium in one of the suburbs. Kurt Tucholsky describes this typically Basque game very accurately in his "*A Pyrenees Book*". But we still don't understand it. To us it seems like an oversized version of ancient squash. Although once you figure out a set of rules you can get just as excited as the enthusiastic audience.

The fact that Barbara just happened to have taken a Spanish course half a year ago – when we had no idea about this journey – seems like a particularly kind move on destiny's behalf. She may not yet be a local, but she can express herself in some way and can understand at least half of the acoustic hieroglyphics flying around us. It is therefore entirely thanks to her that we have neither died of thirst nor hunger and have even mastered special tasks like getting to the Pelote Stadium.

Even though I speak French, can get by in Italian and remember remainders of Latin from school, I just cannot understand a word in Spanish. What is more, they speak so quickly. I can look at them, concentrate and try as hard as I can but what comes out of their mouths remains a mysterious sound to me. Latin is of hardly any use in Spain anyway. For example:

the Latin word "butyrum" leads us understandably to Italian "burro", to French "beurre" to German "Butter". Which makes sense. But the Spanish word for butter is "mantequilla". Which makes no sense to me. But I believe it is hopeless – bananas are called "platanos" here and olives are "aceitunas"…

Puente la Reina, 26 October

From here onwards there is only one Camino de Santiago. In Puente La Reina, "The Queen's Bridge", the beautiful but rarely travelled branch from Arles, joins in with the main route. The more tributaries join together, the stronger the flow and the more powerful the force that draws us to Santiago. Ursula, who was here three days ago, agrees with this: "I spent a restless night here. I'm already beginning to walk slower and slower. Since I have already been travelling for twelve weeks, the remaining stretch to Santiago seems like its almost too short. Ursula (Hof/Bayern -> Santiago)". Well we certainly don't have those fears just yet. After all we still have 680 km ahead of us.

The walk out of Pamplona is not very pretty.

Desert meets agricultural desert, grey and ochre and an unpleasant bright cold light even though the day is quite warm. We keep walking and walking and it almost seems as though every time we turn around Pamplona has snuck up behind us again. It is difficult to shake this city off.

In the church of Zariquiegui we find yet another example of Spanish Catholicism. Even the confessional are separated into male (*hombres*) and female (*mujeres*). Which reminds me that I shouldn't have gone into the toilet labelled M in the bar in Pamplona yesterday.

We spend the evening in the monastery *refugio* with Charles, the older man we first met in Saint-Jean-Pied-de-Port. He is 69 years old and we are pretty sure that he too used "alternative" means to get here this quickly. It just doesn't seem likely that he could have walked 40 km a day, especially now when the days are so short. Charles is very polite. He speaks a little like this: "Dearest Barbara, would it bother you too much to hand me your glass so that I might pour another droplet of this drink of the

116

Gods which goes by the wonderful name of Rioja into it?" There is no irony in this act and it seems rather banal when Barbara replies with a simple "yes please". We just don't have the gift of French flower-iness (which is also found in some French music and architecture as well as cuisine) and I don't think we really regret that. Charles is an old-fashioned French gentleman and so we are hardly surprised to discover that his children and grandchildren are required to use the polite "vous" form when addressing him. "My wife gave in, but even on my deathbed I will demand them to use the polite form," he exclaims with pride.

Estella, 27 October

Today's stint is short and pleasant – only 20 km, of which most are on nice field paths. Charles requested to accompany us. He doesn't look well, possibly because he has exhausted himself, and the idea of walking through the heat and barren landscape on his own was probably too much for him.

So we slowed our pace and walked with him. He

prays a lot while he walks and because it makes him inattentive, he gets lost every few hundred metres. This seems to contradict the popular belief that prayer *stops* you from straying from the right path.

Now that we are in Spain, we come through towns more frequently than in France. Usually one can see them from afar, which helps to speed up the pace. It is nice to be working towards a new goal every once in a while, because it motivates you to keep going even though the ultimate goal, Santiago, is still so far away.

When we get to the pretty *refugio* in Estella in the evening, we find a new message from one of our "acquaintances". Marco has returned to his laconic salute: *pax et bonum* and there is no sign of Ursula. Has she given up?

Although the *refugio* here is very large and clean, the rules, like in all Spanish towns, are very strict. We are locked in at ten and are released at eight the next morning. In between one is held in protective custody, so as not to be found by thieves, terrorists or the homeless. I know it is meant well, but it still doesn't make me feel very comfortable. (During the summer, the opening times are different. Most people leave the hostel around six in the morning in order to arrive at the end of their stint before the afternoon heat.)

Charles decides to join us on our little tour of the town. Estella is certainly worth seeing because it is very charming. There is a Romanesque royal palace, a late Romanesque church named San Pedro de la Rua as and the Iglesia de San Miguel, whose altar shines with lavish magnificence in a bright spotlight. This is even too much for Charles who exclaims: "Look at all this gold and silver, and at what price it was brought here! One might as well fill the church with blood."

Los Arcos, 28 October

Today was a beautiful and pleasant day. Behind Estella, the path splits in two and it is highly recommendable to take the road to Irache. There you will not only find a wonderful monastery and church which are surrounded by the morbid charm of slow disintegration but also a wine cellar which has opened

119

a wine source just for pilgrims. There are two taps coming out of the wall: one for water and one for red wine. The pilgrims who pass through can fill a few sips of what they require into their water bottles. This is a nice gesture of the "Bodegas Irache" and also a great PR stunt, because the wine tap with their logo on it is the second most photographed image on the route after the cathedral in Santiago.

Charles was already waiting for us next to the wine tap. Instead of walking slower we walked at our own pace today, but made sure we turned around ever so often to check whether he was still there. We also got a taste of what the desert-like Meseta would be like when we crossed a wide barren stretch of land without any villages or wells. I was reminded of my grandfather's words: "Lots of area here." Which is exactly what it was and on top of that it was very hot, astonishing for October. It is apparent that Charles is normally cared for by "domestics" (as he calls them) or his wife. He is wearing velour trousers, and undershirt, a t-shirt, a flannel shirt and a jacket. He is sweating so hard that water is dripping off of his nose. When we suggest that he could take his jacket off, he is as excited about this idea as one might be if we had just invented the wheel.

At lunch, we save him again. Instead of water, he has milk in his water bottle, which as we all know is not used to quench thirst but to feed calves to make them strong. Instead of the usual foodstuffs he is carrying kilos of chocolate caramel bars and various other sweets. Fortunately, we filled a small bottle with wine in Irache and a large bottle with water at an early gothic fountain named "Fuente de los Morso" near Villamayor, which makes Charles extremely happy. So we feed him water, wine, bread, cheese, Serrano ham and chorizo sausage. As a thank you, he promises to include us in his prayers, and more importantly gives us a bottle of cognac with which we are to toast to him in Santiago.

In the afternoon we begin to worry about Charles because of his problems with his blood pressure and his heart. But we still want to keep going at our own pace, so we keep looking back to check on him, but suddenly he is gone. We are already beginning to wonder whether he is still all right when we see him drive past us steering a tractor, waving to us. A farmer took pity on him, and let him take the only seat, as driver, leaving himself on the wing.

Los Arcos seems to be unremarkable to us but not unappealing. The official *refugio* is already closed in late October so the place we end up staying is a cross between a pilgrim hostel, a pig-sty, a private room and a gardening site. The good thing is we can come and go as we please.

Our daily routine has fallen into place like this: breakfast around eight, leave between eight and nine (when it gets light) and walk quite quickly because it is cold. In the morning we still talk quite a lot, with topics ranging from our various aches and pains for example (every day), to the stint ahead, to calls from home… Around ten we have a coffee if we are passing through a village or we eat a banana. Then we keep walking and have lunch between twelve and one. If it is raining we do this in a town but our preference is to sit outside somewhere. After that we normally walk a lot slower, one behind the other, in silence which is a pilgrim's siesta. Our thoughts rest or wander at this point. We both find it very difficult to think any topic through properly. The things running through our minds are more like trailers of various films; scattered daydreams, usually pleasant, usually useless. If we find a town in the afternoon, we then have an afternoon coffee. Later we move into our *refugio*, shop, cook something small or go to eat tapas in a local restaurant. Chat, read, write, sleep. We also enjoy reading the Spanish newspapers in bars, because we understand them a lot better than high-speed spoken communication. However, the weather forecast for tomorrow isn't very motivating, predicting *"precipitations debiles"*. This does not mean that it will rain stupid amounts, but that there will be "light precipitation".

Logroño, 29 October

Dinner in Los Arcos yesterday was almost like slapstick. Anyone who has seen "Fawlty Towers" will be able to imagine what I mean. First of all, the cook had to be woken to make us food, and he wasn't just sleepy, but obviously hung over. Since the waiter didn't turn up for his shift, the poor cook also had to serve us. On top of that, the tables from the day before hadn't been cleared yet, so the three of us sat in among the wreckage while the cook, who was wearing an adventurously dirty apron, brought us bits and bobs out of his surprise menu of leftovers from the fridge – a few leaves of lettuce, a can of tuna, a piece of meat that was elegantly cut into three pieces and the obligatory soggy French fries of which there were more than enough to go around. We remained the only guests in the restaurant throughout our stay. To top it all off, we had the privilege of hearing Charles tell us about the virtues of the French Foreign Legion.

The next morning while we were having breakfast at a petrol station buffet, since there are no other open bars in Los Arcos, Charles bleakly commented: "Spanish slaves worked so well under Roman command, but now what has become of this country after the collapse of the Roman Empire? I'm telling you René, you the Teutons and we the Gauls have

the mission to lead Europe into the shining future."
Altruistically, we suggest that he take the bus for a
few kilometres since the stint to Logroño might end
up being too difficult for him. He gratefully accepted
this suggestion as a "permission to cheat" ticket.

Nonetheless our wish for a quiet day didn't come
true. We spent the first two hours walking through a
swampy area permanently being attacked by highly
organised swarms of mosquitoes. Although we were
covered with bites, we were incredibly quick. It was
the first time we ever underbid the time written in
our pilgrim guide, which seems to have been written
by an Olympic sprinter.

We are consoled by our lunch under almond
trees – almonds really taste the best when they come
straight from the tree. But as we pointed out to
Charles, the route is really very long. Thank God the
black patches in the sky remain innocuous and we are
protected from the *"precipitaciones debiles"*.

The suburbs of Logroño are real slums: miserable
corrugated iron huts, dirt, chickens in living rooms,
chained-up dogs, TV aerials, and meagre children with

sad eyes. Amidst all this lives an old lady who is also a "legend" on the route. No one gets by her without being stamped. (Collecting stamps seems to be the most popular activity for pilgrims. One could almost think they are going on a rubber stamp search instead of a pilgrimage.) As indicated on the stamp, the lady gives everyone "water, figs and love" and likes to take pesetas for it in return. In her book we see that Ursula was here two days ago and Marco three days ago (*pax et bonum*).

We are pretty exhausted when we cross the bridge over the broad Ebro river (latin *Iberus*) which gives the Iberian peninsula its name.

Logroño, 29 October
Dear Michi!
It sounds promising – we are currently walking through the "Rioja" province and I fear we have no choice but to get a little drunk on the local wine tonight. At the moment we are sitting in a Laundromat in a suburb and everyone is staring at us. Particularly René is being ogled because he is sitting there dressed only in boxers waiting for his washing

just like the guy in that jeans advert, but with fewer muscles.

The *refugio* here in Logroño is more like a prison. Don't get me wrong, it is very clean and even our reception by the "hospitalero", which is the name for former pilgrims who volunteer to take care of *refugios*, was very friendly. But the hostel already closes at nine in the evening and now it is eight and our clothes are only just on the spin cycle. I wonder how the pilgrims here ever have dinner, since they have to be in the hostel at exactly the time when the restaurants open. I'm not surprised so many people go through Logroño by bus and spend the night in Viana instead. They really aren't missing anything.

I've just put the washing into the dryer and don't feel very good about it. Our sleeping bags are still completely soaked and the beds in the *refugio* are covered with plastic and there are no blankets provided.

One Hour Later
Our sleeping bags are still wet. And the rest of our clothes are annoyingly moist. There is only one dryer

127

in the entire Laundromat and it has turned out to be a congregation point. So we had to wait. But we couldn't because we had to get back to the hostel. So René put on his wet trousers and his damp t-shirt and we packed the rest of the washing into black bin bags and ran back through the streets of Logroño. People crossed to the other side of the street when they saw us approaching and two of the people we wanted to ask for direction ran away entirely. I suppose they thought we were homeless, which we really would have been had we not run fast enough.

Now we are sitting in a sterile kitchen with nice messages stuck to the walls (You must wash up the plates. You have to leave at 8 in the morning) and are drinking Rioja. We aren't drinking to help us fall asleep, because we know that won't be possible. We are drinking because we want to overcome our fear of sleeping in damp clothes on a plastic mattress. It has only just occurred to us that we could have taken a hotel, but it's too late for that now, as we are locked in. Isn't it astonishing how quickly one can go from being homeless to being a prisoner?

One Night Later

Our first few hours of sleep were actually not bad at all. The only problem when we woke up around two in the morning was that we were hung over and victims of yet another snoring contest. A Belgian and two Spaniards were fighting it out with noises I can hardly describe. We finally fell asleep again some time in the morning. The Belgian must have taken that time to add the final touches to our washing disaster when he smoked three cigarillos in the kitchen where our clothes and sleeping bags were drying. Now all of our clothes are coated in the scent of cigars and we have to go because the sign has told us to.

Lots of love, Barbara.

Najera, 30 October

Logrono isn't any better in the sunshine the next day. A lot of the route toward Najera runs along the N 120, which is popular motorway along which many lorries rush past us. What makes these smelly monstrosities even more irritating is that they will reach the goal we have been trying to get to all day within nine minutes. But the original route of the Camino is important to the Spanish and therefore we must stick to the motorway. Maybe this doesn't have anything to do with their fanaticism for historical accuracy but with the fact that people walking in Spain are unlucky as it is. The fact that walking is a luxury for the privileged hasn't yet been fully understood because there are still too many people who have to walk because they have no other choice.

On the wall of the Navarrete graveyard, there is a plaque commemorating the cycling pilgrim Alice de Craemer who died in a road accident in 1986. We are almost surprised there aren't more accidents since we frequently have to cross the large road behind sharp curves and other dangerous stretches. Even though we hate the excessive amount of signs and rules in our country, we would be very happy about slightly more rigorous signposting here. As often as possible we follow the route in our guide instead of the path along the N 120. We make several long detours, but in the end we are less exhausted then those who took the official route.

Najera is positioned beautifully between sand coloured rock faces and the *refugio* is also very pretty, with several floors and many beds – fortunately, because today there are 15 pilgrims spending the night. This may be pathetic compared to the summer, but for late October it is a lot. There is an orderly turnover in the kitchen, toilet and bathroom. There are two Brazilians, two women from Quebec, Charles, who is going home tomorrow, five Spanish "weekend pilgrims" who are taking the trip in bits, and two French pilgrims who are on their way back from Santiago. They are two young unemployed people who instead of sitting around at home have turned walking into their philosophy and have already been walking the route for months. They are real veterans of the Camino and tell us their stories with such self-importance one might think that they themselves invented the Camino de Santiago. They fight over and over again because each of them thinks he is the greater expert. One thing however remains clear to us: walking the route several times doesn't necessarily make you a wiser person.

I don't get enough chances to write because we spend our evenings debating. The Belgian is named Willy and is a professor of comparative sociology, specialising in Shamanism. He speaks German just as well as French and reveals many exciting connections to us. He explains that walking brings out the nomad in all of us, since in the past all of humanity was nomadic. Since that unfortunate story of Abel, the nomadic shepherd, and Cain, the settled farmer, humanity had divided and begun to scorn the small nomadic remnant (like for example the gypsies, the Touaregs or the Kurds, who wherever they go are persecuted by governments). All religious founders were nomadic, pilgrims who described their teachings as a path and not a standpoint. The Shaman, in Africa, Asia and America, also walked many thousand kilometres on foot when they were on a search for visions. The professor adds that the Camino itself is older than Christianity. He saw its roots in heathen shamanism. Santiago had been one of the most important Celtic necropolises, a holy burial ground, positioned in the far west of the continent, where the sun sets, in death.

The name itself may even point to this idea, since it could possibly be derived from *compostum* or graveyard. There are many sanctuaries along the route and next to every chapel or church there was and sometimes still is a grave-mound, a dolmen or a spring. Later Gnostic traditions, perhaps initiated by the Knights Templar, took on the route, even though it had always been the pilgrimage path of the heretics. Only since religious wars had made it difficult to walk to Jerusalem, did Santiago acquire such importance among Catholics.

Santo Domingo, 31 October

We are sitting in a bar in Santo Domingo and all around us there are people singing, dancing and making music who have already been parading around town with drums and trumpets all evening. They are wearing neck scarves that read "Quintada de los 55", 1943–1998". On this day everyone who has turned 55 in 1998 is celebrating. There is no real reason for these festivities. They are just celebrating for the sake of celebrating. It is lovely to watch the crowd and listen to their songs. The old cliché that the Spanish are masters of "fiesta" is proving to be true. We have rarely seen such a contagiously happy group of people who are light and fun and not weighed down by alcohol and the duty of acting carefree like at home.

Today we have taken a room in a kind of "monastery-hotel". I wouldn't have been able to face another night with Willy, no matter how interesting his stories are. You must know that he not only snores loudly, but also irregularly with his mouth wide open which makes it even harder to fall asleep. And yet when he suddenly stops, I'm certain he has just died and that adds to my restlessness.

The stint to Santo Domingo is short and sweet and so we had enough time and energy to take a tour of the town. The cathedral is really worth seeing. There are two chickens living in it inside a glass shrine. The rooster even crowed when we were looking at him and that means good luck. The story with the chickens is derived from a legend. There was once a young man on a pilgrimage to Santiago with his parents. On a break in Santo Domingo, the daughter of a hostel owner fell in love with him. When he turned her down that night, she took revenge on him by hiding a silver cup in his baggage. When it was found he was accused of being a thief and hanged. (Alex Sorbas later taught that one should never turn down loving women.) The desperate parents continued on to Santiago and there Saint James, the patron saint of pilgrims, told them that their son was still alive. On the way back, they stopped in Santo Domingo and went to speak to the judge who was just eating a large portion of poultry. Disdainfully the judge responded: "Don't disturb me during my meal. Your son is about as alive as the chicken and rooster on my plate!" In that very moment, the chicken began to flap its wings and the rooster began to crow, so the judge got up and went straight to the gallows. Lo and behold, the son was still alive and could be saved.

No one knows what happened to the historical chickens afterwards, but the ones in the church today are exchanged once a week. After all, living in a shrine is certainly more comfortable than living in a battery.

Belorado, 1 November

Neither of us has ever cooked on a theatre stage before. The *refugio* in Belorado is situated in an old theatre so we both experience this for the first time in the stage-kitchen. Before televisions were introduced, regular performances took place here. But even a group of pilgrims can be quite a spectacle. The lady from Quebec is here, as well as the five Spaniards and the Belgian and we are all circling the old-fashioned gas stove between bits of washing that we have hung on makeshift washing lines to dry.

Ursula was also here two days ago and from what we can tell from her entry in the guestbook she also thoroughly enjoyed the atmosphere in the theatre after a horrible stint. The official road goes along the N 120 for 19 km – asphalt, dust, noise, trucks, speeding cars. We took a detour that led us through lonely villages south of the motorway. At first we thought these towns were all completely deserted. We sat and ate cheese, bread and olives by a fountain in Viloria de Rioja and it was the warmest first day of November I think I have ever experienced. Suddenly the church bells began to ring. Almost simultaneously people came out of all doorways in their best clothes and headed to mass. So there *is* life in Viloria! A few men remained outside the church smoking and laughing and the bells had to ring three times before they finally went inside. I suppose some remain schoolboys all their lives.

People here are poor, and that is not only revealed by the extravagance of their Sunday dress. The poorer a country, the more important the Sunday dress is. All of the houses are dilapidated, there are hardly any new buildings or developments, and even if, they are incomplete. The dogs are scrawny, the chickens dirty and somewhere in a back room there must be pigs hidden, because it smells of them. There is rubbish lying around everyone, both in the towns and in the fields. I have never found it this easy to not throw my tissues in a bin – it just feels like it doesn't matter anyway. The rivers often look like sewage canals and there are only small remains left of what used to be large forests. The fact that we saw beautiful oak tree groves yesterday only goes to show that it *is* possible for trees to flourish and boost the water supply here. But it seems that people are thinking in a different direction: there are many marvellous new roads that connect these fading villages. This is probably referred to as the promotion of infrastructure and was coined in some big offices in Madrid or Brussels. These roads end in no-man's-land and are only driven upon by lost tourists. The locals who can even afford a car have already moved as far away as possible.

Hornillos del Camino, 2 November

The next morning in Belorado it is raining cats and dogs. A strange epidemic seems to have broken out amongst our co-pilgrims. With the exception of the woman from Quebec, no one wants to walk today. For one, yesterday's stint was exhausting and for another we didn't sleep very well because the Belgian was there and because sometimes exhaustion makes it even harder to fall asleep. After all, we have been on the road for five whole weeks. Added to that the pouring rain isn't exactly inviting us to go outside and get on with it. Moreover, the medieval pilgrims often travelled some stretches on horseback or in a cart.

Within a few minutes we are sitting in the bus to Burgos. On one hand are quite happy about this because we really are shattered. The long walks have left their marks on us in the form of chronic hip pain. On the other hand, we are sad to have missed such a nice stint and most of all the monastery and church of San Juan de Ortega. It is located in a secluded pine wood. We have been told that the priest invites the pilgrims to have garlic soup with him in the evenings. But it continues to rain all day, so we are glad to watch the driving rain from inside the heated bus and a café in Burgos.

We don't like Burgos at all. It feels cold and self-important. The cathedral is darkly gothic and filled with conspicuous amounts of gaudiness. In it we happen to witness the funeral of the 90-year-old Archbishop of Burgos. Behind the coffin is a procession of first the clergy, then the military and then the politicians – a reflection of their respective status within the Spanish social system? Either way, one can still tell that Burgos was the seat of Franco's government during the Spanish Civil War. Even though it is still raining, we don't want to stay. Since our experience in Logrono we have been trying to avoid the hostels in bigger cities. As much as we want to rest, "Camino Real", the royal path between Burgos and Leon, is calling us. Now the Meseta, a plateau feared for its aridity and solitude, awaits us. We can't see or feel the dryness anywhere. We walk through hammering rain in a hurricane-like headwind. Wet to the bone we arrive in the village of Hornillos del Camino at dusk. The *refugio's* hospitalera takes pity on us and gives us some wood to heat the stove with. That way we can try to dry our clothes and warm ourselves up a little. We leaf through the guestbook and delight in the many messages left in the summer complaining about the dreadful heat and thirst they experienced. "We just made it here with our very last drop of energy!" "A kingdom for a coca cola!" Underneath that: "A coca cola for the horse!" There is also a little sketch of a man dying of thirst and the word "waaaaater!" written underneath. It must be lovely to know what heat feels like, we muse, and edge a little closer to the stove.

Castrojeriz, 3 November

The Meseta is an unwelcoming patch of earth. We spent all day fighting the icy headwind and wet chewing-gum-like clay that was forming under our feet and making them stick to the ground. We walked in silence, one behind the other because every word uttered in the endless expanse seemed to die away unheard. It made me think of a story that Guy-Marie, the Canadian, had told us in France. One of his acquaintances had suffered a heart attack whilst crossing the Meseta. He had felt extremely sick and dizzy but had kept on dragging himself along because he didn't want to get left behind in the wasteland. The heart attack was only diagnosed afterwards and the doctor explained that walking had kept his circulation going and consequently saved him. The doctor was so impressed by this narrow escape from death that in the following year he walked the route himself. Yes, those were the kind of stories I was thinking of and I began to notice that I was also feeling a bit dizzy... A little weakness? And my heart? Wasn't it beating slightly irregularly? It happens more often then one thinks... Do I have to sit down for a while? Drink a sip of water? Better not, just keep going... Who knows if I'll ever get up again if I stop now? I look around – nothing but earth and horizon. I look up – dark clouds and two vultures. Suddenly there is a town, which I only see once it is right in front of me – Hontanas. Here, the villages cower in hollows to protect themselves from the wind that fanatically sweeps across the plane. Unfortunately we can't find an open bar in Hontanas, just a shivering dog and a black widow.

Arriving in Castrojeriz isn't much better. The town is distinctly gloomy and dead. All of the façades are crumbling, some houses half collapsed. There is no one on the streets, which is no surprise in this weather. We trudge through the narrow streets. Out of the corners of my eyes, I feel like someone is staring at us. There are two skulls gaping down at us from the top of the Santo Domingo church as if they wanted to curse us.

Apparently the Meseta is challenging for everyone. We have rarely seen a guest book with as many "mystical" entries as in Castrojeriz. All statements revolve around adversity and fears, crises and pain, God and the world. People speak of great sadness and great gratitude for being taken into the *refugio*. The desert makes everyone think in metaphysical terms. It's not surprising that the monotheistic world religions sprung from the desert.

One of the Brazilians is here. He is completely exhausted and lying on his bed looking pale with feverish eyes. He looks a little like Ronaldo when he missed his penalty shot. "One takes everything so personally as a pilgrim," he says. "When the wind blows in my face all day long I scream at the heavens above – Do you have a personal problem with me, God?!"

The truth is: We have a personal problem with God.

We too lie down and fall asleep exhausted until twilight.

Astorga, 6 November

After that, one of the "miracles of the path" that are really only miracles when they happen to you, happened to us. After our day in the Meseta we were once again completely worn-out. In Moissac it was Barbara who had seriously contemplated going home and now it was me. I told myself that I could easily finish the journey in springtime, knowing full well that I would be far too busy then. But I just couldn't face the rain, and the freezing *refugios*, and the pain in my hips and knees and most of all the endless breadth of the Meseta, which literally sucks the energy out of you, particularly if you come from an Alpine country...And what is more, from here onwards, the path would run all the way to Leon either directly next to the motorway or on a man-made route. My will had been broken. I believe it was Schopenhauer who said: "Man can *do* whatever he wants to but he cannot *want* whatever he wants to."

On the way to dinner we met a man in the front room of the Castrojeriz *refugio* who greeted us kindly in French. We began talking and found out that Jean-

Pierre had walked part of the route last year and now wanted to show his wife the Camino. He said he was glad to meet us and if we joined him for dinner he could finally show his wife some "real" pilgrims.

We accepted his offer and ate with Jean-Pierre and Simone. They are about 50 years old, from a town near Bordeaux and immediately likeable. Jean-Pierre is a doctor, which is very convenient. We have been wondering for a while whether it is reasonable to keep walking against the body's will for so long. He lets us describe our symptoms, asks questions and says that a short break would be very good for our joints. He makes a suggestion: we could give them our rucksacks tomorrow and they would bring them to the Ermita San Nicolas in their car, where we could then meet up for lunch. On the condition, of course, that we trusted them with all our possessions.

We would gladly do so.

The hospitalero of Castrojeriz, a bearded, apostle-like figure, wakes us at seven in the morning with coffee and baroque music. A little later we have a second breakfast with our new-found benefactors and are soon on our way, feeling particularly carefree. Everything seems much friendlier today. Walking without a rucksack is like being on holiday. When we get to Ermita San Nicolas, our acquaintances are already waiting for us. The *refugio* here is already closed for the winter. In the main season it is tended to by the Confraternita di San Giacomo di Perugia. The Italian hospitaleros wash the feet of every pilgrim who arrives. "No one could bear it," Jean-Pierre says. "We aren't used to holy actions anymore. By the way," he added "the stretch from here to Fromista hasn't much to offer, but in Fromista there is one of the most beautiful Romanesque churches you will see along the route. It is also a fantastic example of the art of restoration. We don't want to stop you from walking, but why don't you let us give you a lift to Fromista. We can go see the church and then have lunch together…" So it happened. After our picnic Jean-Pierre said: "The path to Carrion de los Condes goes along the main road all the way…it really isn't a nice stint that awaits you tomorrow. I don't want to stop you from walking, but why don't you…"

We spent three days like that. The Honda turned into the "pilgrim mobile", we recovered nicely and Simone and Jean-Pierre became real friends. When we said goodbye in Hospital de Orbigo we hugged each other with tears in our eyes. We walked over what seemed an endless Roman bridge and kept turning around to wave to them. Now we finally know what is meant when others talk of "angels of the route".

We didn't see as many beautiful historical monuments one our whole trip as we did in those two days with them: the church of Santa Maria de la Victoria in Carrion de los Condes (this happens to be the place that was supposed to be Columbus' reward for discovering America); San Tirso and San Lorenzo in Sahagun; the former Cistercian cloister at Mansilla de las Mulas, which unites Romanesque, Gothic and Renaissance that also houses a rococo altar whose ugliness the 87-year-old woman who showed us around couldn't denounce enough times; San Miguel de la Escalada, a mozarabic Minster which was a true masterpiece of sublime ease; the Romanesque Cistercian monastery in Gradefes where the nuns were just beginning to sing their afternoon prayers when we entered. And how wonderful all those carefree walks through Leon were – which to us was the prettiest town on the Camino; the beautiful windows of the gothic cathedral, when the sun came shining in; the stunning church of San Isidore and the world-famous frescoes in the cross vault of the Romanesque Panteon Real, where we wondered what exactly our generation is leaving behind for humanity... We would have missed all of this on foot, because one rarely makes detours voluntarily and in the evening one is normally too tired to go sightseeing.

Well rested and motivated we are back on our way in Hospital de Orbigo.

Astorga, 6 November
Dear Michi!
Our travel statistics have become greatly confused in the past few days (see René's notes). Simone and Jean-Pierre, with whom we spent such pleasant days, are such lovely and warm people. Sometimes they even manage to move themselves to tears. Once, Jean-

Pierre was telling a wonderful and complicated story about something that happened while he was walking the Way last year. It was about two men who coincidentally met in one of the *refugios* but had actually been raised by the same foster mother in Switzerland during the Second World War. When Jean-Pierre described how the two fell into each others arms after fifty years, crying, he and his wife were also quietly weeping. It wouldn't have taken much for us to start crying too.

We had a real vacation from our pilgrimage. It was such a nice change to not walk during the daytime and to be able to sleep in the night time, in real hotels with warm water, soap, and towels. Once, we even had a TV, but on this occasion René had to watch Graz lose about 18:1 against Real Madrid (if I understood correctly).

Now we are in Astorga, which has an overloaded cathedral in the centre and a bishop's palace right next to it. This tasteless, hideous, new romantic structure was built by Antonio Gaudi, even though he was normally a good guy. We found shelter in a small run-down guesthouse because – can you believe it – the *refugio* was full! Swiss, Canadian, Brazilian, Spanish and French pilgrims... more than twenty altogether!

We are eleven or twelve days away from Santiago and if I'm honest, I don't feel particularly sad that our journey is coming to an end. Instead I am a little impatient to get back home and move into our new home, show my face at the office, earn some money... Some people begin walking and never want to stop. In my case, walking has domesticated me. I long to do the laundry, make the beds, cook nice food and do all those things that never really interested me before. But maybe that will change again.

Lots of love, Barbara.

Rabanal, 7 November

We truly enjoyed the path between Astorga and Rabanal. We finally leave the drab fields behind and enter some pine forests. The mountains are finally coming closer, which makes us feel good after so many hopelessly endless plains. Right before Rabanal, the usual yellow arrows point us on a small detour where we see the ancient "pilgrim's oak", a tree with a trunk so large the two of us cannot reach around it together.

We also felt a little bit homesick today because we know that our friends will all be gathered together around a warm stove and feast on the traditional Martini-goose tonight.

Rabanal del Camino is a pretty, quiet mountain village with a nice atmosphere. We feel at home here immediately. Luckily, the *refugio* is also very pleasant, with a fireplace, new showers and wool blankets. There is also another *refugio* here that is run by a British order, which is said to be the nicest on the whole route... but the English have already left the region.

Rabanal is a good example for the towns on the Camino that are really blossoming due to the new-found popularity of pilgrimages. Rabanal was once the seat of the Templar order and one of the most important hospices on the Spanish part of the Way. A few years ago there was no sign of this. In 1989 the pilgrim Hans Aebli noted in his book *"Santiago, Santiago"*: "The main road of Rabanal del Camino was alive when pilgrims used to come through here. Now it is dead." Ten years later, Rabanal has not one but two *refugios* and a hotel with a bar and an excellent restaurant.

Almost all of the pilgrims from the hostel in Astorga are here today. Everyone is speaking a mixture of English, French, Spanish and German – a kind of pilgrim's Esperanto. The main topics are, as always: how do I get my rucksack to be lighter, what might be waiting for us in the next few days, who is hurting where.

Rabanal, 7 November
Entry in the guest book
Dear Ursula!
We are two pilgrims from Austria. We left Le Puy on the September 23rd and soon after we began to find your notes in various hostels: in Livinhac where you were on your own and decided to clean the *gîte d'étape* (thank you) or in Cajarc where you warned us not to

walk the wrong route that you had... Anyhow, we feel like we already know you quite well and would have loved to actually meet you in person. But when we were having our pilgrim crisis in the plains near Leon, two car-pilgrims picked us up and gave us a ride. Now it seems we must have overtaken you. Nevertheless, we would be so happy to hear from you again so we have left you our address and maybe you could send us yours so that we can write to you. We wish you a wonderful remaining journey to Santiago. Ultreïa! René and Barbara.

Molinaseca, 8 November

In the morning, the hostel has turned into a hospital: one swollen knee, one inflamed ankle ligament and two complaints of nausea. As a result, most of the pilgrims stay to rest another day. As usual, only the older pilgrims are fit and ready to go, and luckily we are too.

It is very foggy and the ground is covered with a thick layer of frost. This isn't surprising since Rabanal is located at 1150 m above sea level. The first hours of our trip are spent climbing upwards to the famous "Cruz de Ferro" at 1490 m. It is a small iron cross on a high wooden pole under which lie thousands of little rocks, a rubble dump of the past. The tradition is that every pilgrim leaves behind a stone that he has brought along – preferably from home – and with it symbolically leaves something that he would like to be rid of. This practice is much older than Christianity, since it was the Romans who already recorded the custom of carrying a stone to the "Monte Mercurio". When we arrive at the Cruz de Ferro the sun is just breaking through the wall of fog. The highest point is also the weather divide. From here on it becomes continually warmer and friendlier.

We spend the first hours walking with Paul from Poland who is wearing heavy Austrian hiking boots and carrying 26 kilos on his back and is still a lot faster than we are. Paul has so little money that he collects old bread that others have left behind in the *refugio*. Most pilgrims come from wealthy countries, because they can afford to seek out an impoverished lifestyle.

Later we are joined by Jim, a pilgrim from New York State, who draws the American flag onto a full page in every hostel and writes underneath: "One pilgrim representing the United States of America". We find out from talking to him that he is actually looking for a woman to settle down with on the Camino and he is very disappointed that he hasn't yet found her, even though he is already so close to Santiago.

There are quite a few sites along this mountainous path. For example, the Knight Templar Tomás, who is the very last inhabitant of the dilapidated village of Manjarin. He has nailed together some boards to build a hut and on top there is a flag with the Templar cross flapping in the wind. It is an old tradition, that upon entering, the pilgrim bell is rung. Inside the hut there are four puppies snuggled up against the stove, bacon and garlic hanging from the ceiling and there is a picture of knights on the wall and an enormous old sword. On a ledge there is a golden cup, no doubt a symbol for the Holy Grail. Every pilgrim is allowed to stay in this strange *refugio* as long as he wants and eat and drink as much as he wants to. Everything is free of charge. Tomás lives only from donations. Every morning he has a praying ritual where he begs for the divine protection of all pilgrims on the route. He considers himself to be the last guardian of the tradition of Knights Templar who used to protect the pilgrims from robbers, wolves and marauders. Although there aren't any looting soldiers and robbers anymore, wolves do still come here frequently, says Niko from Hoyerswerda. He is learning the Templar business as a squire and is helping to upgrade the hut in preparation for the predicted increase of pilgrims in 1999. Niko brews coffee for us and explains what it means to be a Knight Templar. One must live a simple and relatively impoverished lifestyle, since money and luxuries only distract from the essential: from prayer, mystical experiences of God and active compassion for others.

The official guardians of the pilgrim route don't think much of Tomás. It appears that the Catholic Church, which has always been suspicious of those things that are truly Christian, has forced the mayor in charge to cut Tomás off from the power and telephone lines. To overcome this, he has acquired a small diesel generator which is used very sparingly. Niko tells us that it is particularly hard in the winter, since there is so much snow, and the wolves come closer and closer and try to steal their chickens every day.

After an hour we said goodbye to the knight and his squire. The two are, of course, romantics, but maybe this is better than being enlightened and modern like we are. They have the "look of magic". I can still see their eyes clearly in my mind today.

It is becoming warmer and warmer. In El Acebo we even drink our delicious coffee sitting in the sun outside. The vegetation is changing too. The six foot broom yields to enormous chestnut trees which have distributed themselves in circles in some fields, thus making excellent picnic locations.

Sitting under such a chestnut tree in a tent made from old plastic sheeting is Balbino, waiting for pilgrims, for no apparent reason. Balbino is about 70 years old, looks like Anthony Quinn, wears a filthy Nike baseball cap and gives us chestnuts that he has roasted over his camp fire. He asks us whether there are still many more pilgrims to come after us. When we say no, he accompanies us. On a small high ground he stops us and tells us to look into the distance – "See," he says, "that down there is my Molinaseca!"

He loves his town for a good reason. We stride over the Romanesque pilgrim's bridge and feel well immediately. It seems that Molinaseca is particularly "in" at the moment. All of the bars and restaurants are full and the streets are parked full of cars from Madrid. As usual we order the "menu del peregrino" and as usual the only enjoyable thing is the wine that comes with it.

Vega del Valcarce, 9 November

Today was another day that taught us how useless it is to plan ahead. During our chestnut breakfast in Molinaseca, we would never have thought that we would end up in Vega that evening.

Yesterday's stint over the Montes de Leon into the fertile Bierzo plains was one of the prettiest on the Camino de Santiago. In contrast, today has been somewhat of a letdown. After walking for an hour we arrive in Ponferrada, an industrial city, which hasn't got much to offer other than the remainders of a Templar fort from the 12th century. Since the way out of the city leads along the main road through an industrial estate and seemingly endless suburbs, we decide to take the bus for a few kilometres. In the area around Villafranca ("French Town") wine dominates the vegetation and we breathe in deeply as we continue walking.

Villafranca has one of the most famous *refugios* of the Camino, which is also run by one of the most famous people of the route. It is the *refugio* of Jesus Jato. It consists primarily of plastic and tenting material and has no toilet, water or beds. Instead one has the pleasure of Jesus Jato and his family's company. Jesus is said to be a "Shaman" and there are many legends of him healing even the most ailing pilgrims. He too has benefited from the boom in pilgrimages and proudly presents us his new, luxurious (brick-walled) rooms.

We arrive in Villafranca in the afternoon and

want to keep walking. There are two possible routes to Trabadelo: one leads through the valley along the main road next to which a new motorway is being built and the other involves a steep climb over the top of a mountain on the route marked by Jesus Jato himself. We decide on the latter and don't regret it. Although we nearly lose ourselves in the broom which is growing taller than our heads we spend the next two hours walking through picturesque chestnut forests. We watch an old woman gathering nuts and loading them onto her donkey and see the sun shimmering through the golden leaves. The scenery is so beautiful it seems unreal.

Reality soon catches up with us. In Trabadelo one can really feel the contrast between traditional and modern Spain, between poor and wealthy, between the Middle Ages and modernity. While 20 m away the motorway is filled with hundreds of cars and trucks and another 20 m beyond them, high-tech mechanical diggers are flattening the remainders of nature into the ground a lone farmer is walking down the main street of Trabadelo with two cows in a yoke.

He tells us that they have been working all day and are very tired, but still need to be milked. One of them isn't actually his but has merely been borrowed from his neighbour and tomorrow he will lend his cow to someone else. Cows for working? Donkeys for transport? In the place we come from, the only time you still use a yoke is to decorate an "authentic" chalet restaurant. I suppose it will be like that here soon as well. It can't be long before this town is lost in the shadows of the motorway and only a small service area will remind people of the existence of Trabadelo.

There is even a motel here already. It is called "At the New Street". People didn't use to be proud of developments like this ... We arrive there well after dark and hear the bad news: all the rooms are already occupied by the construction workers and there are no other hotels or hostels in the town. We also know that we cannot walk along the main road at night because it is far too dangerous. So, we ask the owner to call us a taxi and twenty minutes later we are in Vega de Valcarce. The *refugio* is particularly ugly and the food is the same old microwave mush... But we are happy that we have at least got a roof over our heads tonight.

Alto do Poio, 10 November

Today we are embarking on a mythical stint: we are hiking over the 1300 m high Cebreiro to Galicia, into the "Galician", "Celtic" province in north-western Spain. Medieval pilgrims considered Galicia to be somewhat of a holy land since the Cebreiro was the last difficult mountain to cross. One could finally see the green hills in the land of milk and honey. This impression is still easily identifiable nowadays. When we look down into the land from the peaks of the Cebreiro we are filled with confidence because the meadows with little stone walls and strips of forest look so luscious and friendly. From here, we can feel Santiago and walking becomes easy. The holy city seems to draw pilgrims to it like a magnet and it almost takes discipline to stop and rest at night. We have heard of pilgrims experiencing real "walking highs" in Galacia and travelling up to 50 km a day until they nearly collapsed.

162

The ascent is very hard at times. We are glad that the climb is at the beginning of the stretch because we are still feeling fresh and can really enjoy the marvellous landscape that is reminding us more of Ireland with every step.

In the small village of O Cebreiro we treat ourselves to an extensive lunch break in a bar that has been converted from a "palloza" which is a type of old house made of slate. We appreciate the pleasant simplicity of the mountain church of O Cebreira. Inside, there is a golden cup reminding visitors of the miracle that once took place here: Even though there was a snowstorm, a farmer from Barxamajor came to the little church for mass, like every day. The priest looked at him and thought, "What a simpleton he must be to come all this way every single day for a little piece of bread and some water." In that very moment the sacrament turned into flesh, and the wine in the cup into real blood.

Fortunately the wine we are served with our potato stew stays wine. It warms us as we walk and makes the headwind just a little less painful.

We have been told that there is a kilometre countdown to Santiago after O Cebreiro. The numbers are marked every 500 m from 152 km downwards. Although this may be the case, it isn't much help to us because souvenir-hunters have removed almost all of the signs. As a result we have some trouble finding the right path even though this is meant to be the most accurately marked part of the route. We take the route along the road, because there are hardly any cars around anyway.

We walk until we reach Alto do Poio, which is the peak point of our stint at 1337 m. This isn't particularly high and yet we get the impression that earth and sky are becoming one. Perhaps this has something to do with the clouds that are particularly low in this area. We can feel that Europe's weather cauldron, the Atlantic Ocean, is not far from here. Although we can see in every direction, every now and then we are surprised by snatches of clouds that plunge everything into thick fog. The mountains are revealed again very quickly and make way for a red orange sunset: over there lies Santiago.

We get a cheap hotel on the pass with hot water and heating. What more could a November pilgrim want? Unfortunately our evening walk through the town is cut short by the fact that the town consists of two houses. So we cross the street and take a seat in the bar. It has a sensationally old table football, with large figures made of wood with real faces, and an open fireplace with a fire burning inside it.

Samos, 11 November

We awake to a typical Galician morning: thick fog and bucketing rain. This is clearly the reason why Galicia is so green. Our descent from Alto do Poio reminds us of Ireland from both a meteorological and a landscape point of view.

Finally we see the first kilometre signs: 141 km to Santiago. This isn't exactly a short distance on foot, but since we are used to this kind of signposting from driving on the motorway it doesn't seem half bad. 141 km means one hour by car...

In Triacastela we are confronted with Galicia's poverty. In front of the church, a woman begs for food

165

or money to buy food with. The Lugo province in which we find ourselves is the most un-industrialised region in the European Union.

In Triacastela there are two options: either take the official path via San Xil and Calvor to Sarria or to head towards Samos.

In Samos we find the following entry in the hostel's guest book:

"Salut to all of you! First of all: congratulations for choosing the route through Samos instead of the one through Calvor. One really mustn't believe all the travel guides that say the whole stint is along a main road. As you can see, it isn't true, and this irritating mistake is copied from one guidebook into the next. It only proves how badly some authors research their topics! Besides, the path is beautiful and dotted with wonderfully picturesque villages. When you leave Samos, you only have to walk along the road for a few kilometres and then take the route that branches off and is marked very nicely with yellow arrows. It may be longer, but it is also much prettier. If you prefer not to, then you can just keep following the main road like a Parisian civil servant. Either way, I recommend that you take part in either the morning or the evening prayer with the monks so that you get a little taste of what monastery life is like. Ferdinand Soler de Boulogne (Paris/Francia)."

This is a loose translation of the message left by our old friend Ferdinand, whom we first met in the *refugio* in Najera and who is walking the route in the opposite direction. We really cannot add anything to his comments on the beauty of the Camino and the quality of the guide books. San Julián, the Benedictine monastery of Samos, is truly imposing. As often in Spain, one can find all styles represented in this building: Romanesque, Gothic, Classical and Baroque. We are particularly impressed by the fountain in the monastery's courtyard: the breasts of the women holding the upper basin with their delicate arms are astonishingly naturalistic. Something we wouldn't have expected in a monastery at all.

Ferdinand was also right about attending the monks' prayers. There are only 13 Benedictines left in this enormous building and only two of them are relatively young. It is extremely gripping when these few men in dark habits begin singing Gregorian chants at the vespers. When I consider that they do this with the same intensity and precise regularity, twice a day, I almost want to thank them directly for maintaining their "professional" contact with God.

The *refugio* in the monastery is large but frugal. There is a small "meson" opposite it that serves hearty Galician specialties like "caldo gallego", a soup made from pork with beans and cabbage, or "cachola", a kind of stew made from bristly pig's head rinds. One really needs to like this kind of cuisine to enjoy it.

Portomarin, 12 November

The stretch from Samos via Sarria to Portomarin is more than 30 km long, but as promised, very beautiful. The Galician sun, obviously out of character, is shining brightly from the blue skies. The landscape doesn't feel Spanish at all, but increasingly Irish, Scottish or Breton. Suddenly Santiago seems very far away – even though we have already passed the 100 km sign. It seems completely absurd that we have also been 1500 km away from our destination at some point on this journey. But most absurd of all is the idea that we will actually arrive there in three days.

We notice the efforts that have been made by the Galician "Xunta" and even some individuals to justify the current pilgrimage boom. There have been new *refugios* built in many of the small towns (like Barbadelo or Ferreiras) and they offer everything a pilgrim could possibly want. It seems that some farmers have also converted their barns into bars if they are positioned along the route. We stop to have coffee in such a place and can tell immediately that the barman is not particularly familiar with this trade. He asks us just a little too precisely how we would like our coffee (How big? How big exactly? In which cups? How much milk? How much sugar?), only to serve us something completely different after fidgeting around with the brand-new espresso machine excitedly. He lets the coffee run for far too long and then manages to pour the milk on it in such a way that all the foam (the only reason to put milk in your coffee) stays in the metal jug. He places the coffees in front of us with trembling hands and a satisfied look. It is nice to see how easy it is for people here to take the initiative and start their own businesses. At home, we would never be able to sell drinks to someone without the necessary paperwork and permission.

We walk through a lot of water in Galicia. Like the Celts, the Galicians adore springs and brooks and have through the millennia filled the country with artistic irrigation canals named "regos" and "corredoiras". These routes of spring water often lead over the roads, so little walkways have been built next to them out of slate.

"Horreos" are another characteristic feature of Galicia. We find them everywhere along today's stretch. They are stone-walled grain storehouses built on four pillars to protect the harvest (usually corn) from moisture and rodents. Some of these structures are several hundred years old and are historically invaluable.

We already recognise Portomarin, today's goal, from afar. The town feels as artificial as its name. There is hardly any recognisable "porto", and certainly no "marin". At least not anymore. When you walk over the new bridge across the Rio Miño, you can still see the old Roman bridge and remains of the old town far below. When the water is high, the old Portomarin disappears completely. In 1962 this 10th century city had to make way for a reservoir. So it was deconstructed and rebuilt on higher ground. Every single stone in the San Nicolas church still carries a number which allowed it to be reconstructed exactly. It must have been like a giant Lego set. But something must have happened to the church bells along the way, because today people are summoned to mass with baroque music blaring from loudspeakers.

The *refugio* is pretty full for this time of year: there are two cycling pilgrims from Brazil who, like all Brazilians so far, deny that they are taking the trip because of Paulo Coelho whom they consider a terrible writer. ("I have never read him and will never read him" is what all the Brazilians we have met say, and there were quite a few of them. Eventually it turns out that every single one of them only knows about the Camino from the book Coelho wrote.) But back to the *refugio*: there are two Swiss pilgrims who have been walking since Geneva and a French actor who is deliberating over his divorce and the future of his career on the route. Alain tells us that he was on tour with his theatre company a year ago with a play about the Way of St James. At some point the company had dissolved, and he had gone on his way.

Palas do Rei, 13 November

Today is Friday the 13th. As if to mock us, a black cat suddenly turns up during breakfast at the *refugio*. But as we all know: one shouldn't be too superstitious, because it brings bad luck.

It is raining buckets today and on top of it there is a fierce wind. We are the last to leave, hoping that the weather might just improve. But it does not. The stretch seems particularly long to us although it is only 24 km long. Somehow the "countdown" to Santiago is slowing us down, because at every stone we are reminded exactly how long it can take to walk 500 m.

The landscape is becoming more and more open but also losing its appeal. Stone pine and eucalyptus groves dominate the scenery. We have our lunch break on the side of a country road in a plastic bus stop hut. This may be particularly unromantic, but we are safe from the wind and rain.

The name Palas do Rei sounds much more impressive that the town is. It is said that Visigoth king's palace was located here in the 7th or 8th century. We don't find a palace anywhere, but the *refugio* isn't bad either.

Arzúa, 14 November

I'm slowly beginning to feel that we are coming closer to a large city. Towns are appearing more frequently, the houses we see can easily be recognised as second homes and the landscape is becoming less rural.

Today we are lucky with our choice of restaurant (it is called "Venus") and we have a delicious meal. Especially the "pulpo", or giant squid, which is adored by Galicians in an almost cultish way, tastes exceptional. We are now 38 km away from our destination.

We order a glass of wine and begin to draw our first conclusions about the journey – very carefully, of course, since we know we could still fail… One false move, one slip – and the trip could be over. We have realised that there are many things we could have done to ease our difficulties along the way: for one, I only thought of buying earplugs a week ago – I have been able to sleep next to five snorers without a care ever since. Barbara only realised two days ago that she could readjust the straps on her rucksack to move the weight to her shoulders and stop her hip pain immediately. We reminisce about all our stops along the way: Le Puy seems so far away…, we think about all the crises we had, about how much it rained in France, how lucky most of our encounters were, and the transformation everyone talks about? We can't recognise it anywhere. And yet we feel like this pilgrimage has changed something in us. We just cannot find a label for it. And we don't want to either.

We also think about whether we should walk all the way to Santiago tomorrow – 38 km would be achievable. But tradition says that one should arrive in Santiago well rested. We have learned from experience that exhaustion can almost have a paralysing effect in a large city. Consequently we decide that we should take our time and enjoy these last two days.

Arca, 15 November
Dear Michi!

Today we are sitting in a friendly, heated (!) *refugio* in Arca, 20 km from Santiago. It certainly is exciting to be this close to our goal after all this time. We heard from some pilgrims (many are on their way for the second or third time!) that there are wild parties filled with drinking, dancing and celebrating until late along the last stint before Santiago. It is said that the next morning groups of euphoric and slightly hung-over pilgrims make their way into the holy city shouting with joy. We haven't noticed any big emotions like this yet. We would have spent a completely uneventful night in the *refugio* if there hadn't been a group of thirty-two 17-year-old students staying with us. The boys are incredibly loud, but very friendly. Their teacher is a priest from Galicia, who like all Galicians feels Celtic. (Galicia is related to "Gallia". People here also drink cidre (sparkling apple wine) and the national instrument is the bagpipe – like in Brittany, the other Finistère in the west of France. Gallego however, which is spoken in Galicia, is not a Gaelic language, but related to Portuguese.) The priest has invited us to take part in an old Celtic ritual that is supposed to banish evil spirits. It is called "Queimada", which mean "it was burned" in Gallego.

The priest confides in us in English: "I shouldn't really be doing these magic rituals, since I am a priest after all." But we just encouraged him to celebrate his ritual since priests are, after all, obliged to banish evil spirits.

We all went outside. It was a clear starry night and the students carried an enormous cooking pot with two kilos of sugar, five lemons and two litres of schnapps outside. The sugar was poured into the pot and mixed with the lemon juice. Then the priest poured the schnapps on top and then set fire to the entire contents of the pot ladle after ladle with a lighter. He added that "Photography and sound recordings are forbidden since the spell won't work then." I'm sure it had a little more to do with him being confronted with evidence of conducting a heathen ritual as a Catholic priest. Either way, eventually, the whole pot was burning brightly and all the faces surrounding it glowed in a reddish light. We had to memorise a Celtic magic charm that means something like "Evil spirits out! Good spirits in!" On command, this charm had to be called out by the whole group a total of three times while the priest turned the liquid into burning waterfalls with his ladle. Then he said the potion was ready and stuck his finger in, pulling it out in flames and tasting the fire water. The boys squealed like a group of girls and held out their glasses. "Just a moment," the priest said, "first we must serve our guests!" A path cleared for us and we were invited to be the first to taste the still burning potion. It tasted extremely sweet and just one sip was enough to make us drunk. "This potion will carry you to Santiago on wings and you will be protected from all enemies!" was the priest's blessing which the students translated for us. Then the priest apologised to us for the impending noise throughout the night by saying "We are trying to go to sleep now. Please forgive us."

The group wants to depart tomorrow morning in the dark in order to arrive in Santiago for the midday mass. This is the famous pilgrim's mass where a 50-kilo incense burner is swung over the pilgrims by six strong men (it is said that this tradition was introduced to neutralise the smell coming from the pilgrims). We considered joining them but then why rush on the very last day? We saw a commemorative plaque on the path today. Under a strange monument – a pair of bronze trainers – it says: "Guillermo Watt, Pilgrim. Returned to God in his 61st year, one day before Santiago, on August 25 of the holy year 1993."

We are very excited already. Will we like Santiago? Who knows. The only thing we are certain of is that we want to continue on toward the Atlantic coast, which is the real end of the Way because it is the end of the world – "Finisterre".

After that we will already be on our way home! I'm so looking forward to it!

Lots of love, Barbara.

Santiago, 16 November

I am writing the word Santiago with a definite sense of celebration. We have arrived. And suddenly we feel like our pilgrimage has passed very swiftly.

We already felt that this day was extraordinary this morning. It certainly is very special to depart on the last stint of such a long journey and walk the last 20 of more than 1000 km. We are happy.

The route is unspectacular other than the colonies of chanterelle mushrooms which are unexpected in their setting within large eucalyptus forests. What surprised us even more was the sudden deafening noise of an aeroplane landing near us. We knew that the path leads past Santiago International Airport, but had no idea it could be *this* close...

The kilometre numbers are decreasing a little faster than usual today.

All the towns we pass now are closely tied up with

pilgrim traditions. For example Lavacolla, whose name is derived from "lavar", wash, and "cola", tail, suggesting a thing or two about the state of hygiene medieval pilgrims were in. Monte del Gozo, which is now nearly a suburb of Santiago literally means Mountain of Happiness. From here, pilgrims could see the towers of the cathedral of Santiago for the very first time. Today, one cannot see these towers anymore because the view is blocked by skyscrapers. Our first view of the holy city is disappointing: other than a few villas, a lot of apartment blocks and just as many building cranes there isn't much to see.

We take our very last break on the Monte del Gozo, next to the San Marco chapel. We are both lost in thought and stare apathetically at the modern monument reminding of the mass given here by the pope in front of half a million people in 1989.

Of course our entry into Santiago is linked with many expectations. It simply cannot live up to them. We had heard of tears of joy, nocturnal revelry on the Monte del Gozo, hugging between complete strangers and religious ecstasies. It is a little like going to the cinema when too many people have already told you about a fantastic film. When you finally watch it, you feel like you already know it and are necessarily disappointed.

The sign which simply reads "Santiago" as if this meant nothing is positioned along a main road at the end of a bridge over the motorway. Even the loudest exclamation of joy is drowned out by the noise levels here.

The historic city centre begins at the Porta do Camino, and we find ourselves quickly getting lost in its narrow angular alleyways. We still feel very comfortable though, because as far as labyrinths go, it is very pleasant.

Of course our expectations rise, and of course they aren't fulfilled. We hug each other when we arrive in Plaza Obradoiro at the "0" kilometre sign set in the ground in front of the cathedral. But at the same time, it is clear to us that this arrival does not mean very much to us. We walked in order to walk the route. Kilometre 0 doesn't symbolise "deliverance" to us because we never considered this pilgrimage to

181

be a self-inflicted punishment – even if it sometimes seemed like it might turn into one. Ecstasy? Highest spirits? No. What significance as a goal should the opulent cathedral of a powerful saint hold to two non-Catholics like us? No, the goal is definitely not the goal. But one thing is certain: the path is the path. And we are grateful for all the adventures it gave us.

We enter the cathedral through the northern portal, walk around the choir, practically climb into the raised altar to the silver chest which allegedly contains St James's remains, hug the statue from behind according to the tradition and then approach the western portal, the famous Portico de la Gloria. Like millions of pilgrims for thousands of years before us, we place a hand on the middle column where a substantial indentation has formed. Afterwards, we pay our respects to the great architect and sculptor Master Mateo at the pillar in which he purportedly depicted himself, by touching our foreheads against his three times in order to absorb some of his wisdom. Then we stick our hands into the lions' mouths that guard the pillar on each side. Whether this corresponds with the "real" rituals is hard to prove. We simply imitated what others were doing. (David Lodge also describes the ritual at St James's column in his book *"Therapy"*: "Willingly I laid my forehead against the marble head. Not all visitors were completely sure of these rituals. Every once in a while someone would hit his head against the column under the statue and lay his fingers in the groove underneath and promptly several others would follow this example. I would have liked to see whether a Bavarian *schuplattler* would have caused the same imitation effect, but in the end I was too scared to try it out.")

We step out into the open again and leave the cathedral walking west. Tired and satisfied we sit down in front of a café. The tables stand in the evening light, sheltered from the wind. We order tea and Tarta Santiago, a delicious almond cake. Both taste so good that we order another round. Finally we are full and drink the cognac that Charles entrusted us with in Los Arcos, from the little bottle as discreetly as possible. We then find an inexpensive, completely dilapidated room with a view of one of the cathedral's towers.

Santiago, 17 November

The pilgrims' mass that takes place daily at noon in the cathedral of Santiago is the first that we leave before it has ended. It is being monotonously recited in a dead voice by a fat priest who repeatedly coughs into the microphone. He seems to be trying to beat some kind of speed record in praying. Is Santiago also a spiritual freezing point?

We receive our "Authentica", labelling us as real pilgrims, in the town's central pilgrim office. The friendly young lady at the desk admires all of our stamps and checks the dictionary for Latin translations of our names...*Omnibus et singulis praesentes inspecturis, notum facit Barbarum et Renatum Freund hoc sacratissimum Templum pietatis causa decote visitasse...* Everyone who has walked the last 100 km or cycled the last 200 km is entitles to the "Authentica". It entitles the first pilgrims who arrive at the Hostal de los Reyes Catolicos free meals. It is a remarkable Renaissance building which has now been converted into the five-star Parador hotel. We have, however, heard that pilgrims are not permitted in the ornate dining room, but are fed from a separate staff menu in the back rooms. Although we still consider this a kind gesture on the hotel's behalf, the sun is shining so beautifully that we decide to pay for our tapas ourselves in a café on the street.

We feel strange; pleasant but by no means in high spirits. After thinking about this for a while we realise that what we are missing is the walking.

At the End of the World, 17 November

The coach takes a good two hours to get to the End of the World. Dusk is already approaching when we arrive. Finisterre, or Finisterra in Galician, is a small fishing town with a port in which colourful boats bob up and down and a beach with a few palm trees on it. We make our way to the lighthouse that is positioned at the farthest end of the continent. The road leading there is longer than we expected. When we arrive at the lighthouse, after following the blinking signal, it is already pitch black. A new moon. We look over the edge of the cape's cliffs, but we cannot see any water. The abyss is eerie. All we can perceive is the deep, dark, rushing black. There is no doubt about it: we have come to the end of the world.

In the air, 18 November
Night. Descending in Marseilles. I see my face reflected in the window of the small propeller airplane. Unshaven, it almost looks like it could belong to a medieval pilgrim. But I just need to shift my eyes a little and I can see the propeller, the millions of city lights below, the enormous illuminated port, a snake of red lights which must be a traffic jam on the motorway... Just three hours in a plane geographically cancel out two months on foot. What an astounding world we live in.

In our new home, three weeks later
Dear Ursula!
You can't image how happy we were to receive a letter from you. Barbara started dancing around the room shouting: "Guess who wrote to us?!" Of course I couldn't.

I'm so glad you arrived in Santiago safely... More

than 3000 km on foot, that certainly is impressive. We were also very happy to hear that you met up with Marco again at your goal. Your trip to Finisterre together must have been beautiful. It's too bad really, that we didn't take any more time out to do it.

Unlike you, on our arrival in Santiago, we didn't feel like walking back all the way was a tempting thought. Thanks to our "Authentica" the travel agent gave us a 50% pilgrim discount, which made the flight back to our "base camp" in the south of France affordable. Your trip back on the bus with all those breakdowns must have been pretty tiring… Going from Galicia to Bavaria in one week is quite an achievement.

In the meantime we have pretty much re-socialised ourselves. But it does seem that James is following us sometimes. We've only just noticed that the town in which we have been living for five years has a church dedicated to St James and a few minutes walk away from it there is a spring locally referred to as "James's fountain"!

Best wishes (I suppose Ultreïa is no longer appropriate?), Barbara and René

In our new home, two days later
Dear Simone, Dear Jean-Pierre!
Thank you so much for your kind letter. Unfortunately we couldn't provide you with as wonderful a gift as the sparkling stone you gave us from Castrojeriz – which was also so nicely wrapped! You are so lovely!

The route after Ponte de Orbigo, where we said good-bye is absolutely beautiful: Rabanal, Cruz de Ferro and Cebreiro are all definite highlights of the camino.

As promised, we toasted to you in Santiago. A few days later we returned to Austria and it was a bit strange to exchange the sea and palm trees with mountains and 40 centimetres of fresh snow.

You asked how long the route was in total. Well there isn't really a precise answer for that. Even the marked routes have variants which means that even the most accurate pilgrims end up with different kilometre results. In books, the number ranges from 1450 to 1550 km. We were right in between those numbers with 1501 km. 727 of those were in France and 774 in Spain. We walked 1138 km and for various reasons (no available hostel, rain, exhaustion, injury)

188

we travelled 363 km by hitchhiking, bus or in your "pilgrim mobile".

You, Simone, asked how I will go about writing my book. I've been wondering about that too. I just looked through all of my notes, letters, and recordings… It's enough for about three books. I truly re-walk the journey every day that I spend writing, which sometimes makes strange things happen. Sometimes I freeze even though the thermostat is still at 20 degrees and sometimes I get so tired that I fall asleep at my desk. I'm beginning to realise that I every day is stored somewhere inside me and that I re-experience the emotions I had that day when I write them down.

But we haven't told you about the biggest surprise of our trip, because we only found out a few days ago. When we were with you, you weren't just carrying two pilgrims in your car, but three. Although the third was still very, very small. If it's a boy, the name James would be nice, don't you think?

A big hug to both of you,
Barbara and René

Epilogue

All characters in this book are real. To protect their privacy, I have changed some of their names.

I would like to thank...

Barbara, for walking to the end of the world (and back) with me; Natalie, for giving us a base camp and a home; Michi, for supporting us with so many letters; Hermann and Brigitte, for building us a home while we went for a walk; our parents, for letting us learn French; Pati and Heino, for inviting Peter; Peter, for telling us about the Way of St James; all the people who gave us shelter along the way, particularly Aline and Yves in Aire-sur-l'Adour, Xavier in Le Haget; all of our friends from the route, especially Simone and Jean-Pierre, Katharina and Sophie; Ursula and Marco, whom we never met; and last but not least, James, who kept us going.